(Among Friends)

WITH

Heart & Soul

RECIPES BY
Roxie Kelley and Friends

ILLUSTRATED BY
Shelly Reeves-Smith

**Andrews McMeel
Publishing**

Kansas City

Shelly Reeves-Smith and Roxie Kelley

www.andrewsmcmeel.com

03 04 05 RRD 10 9 8 7 6 5

Library of Congress Cataloging-in-Publication Data on file
ISBN: 0-8362-5690-5

ATTENTION: SCHOOLS AND BUSINESSES
Andrews McMeel books are available at quantity discounts with bulk purchase for educational, business, or sales promotional use. For information, please write to: Special Sales Department, Andrews McMeel Publishing, 4520 Main Street, Kansas City, Missouri 64111.

Presented
to:

"A friend may well be
reckoned with a masterpiece
of nature."

~ George Eliot

Dear Friends,

Since the release of "Just a Matter of Thyme", my partner, Shelly Reeves Smith, and I have received so many wonderful letters from people like you who have found our books and cards meeting special needs in your lives. We love hearing from you! But we have felt from the beginning that we would be remiss in accepting your gratitude and praise without, at the same time, mentioning the many employees of "Among Friends" who make it possible for these products to arrive and rest in your gracious hands.

As we considered creating a second cookbook, we knew it would have to include these employees and be dedicated to them, for they really are the "heart and soul" of our business.

At this point in time, there are only thirteen of us. But we are convinced there is more energy, passion and spirit within this small group than in the largest of corporations. No where else will you find a group of people who represent such a wide range of educational backgrounds and talents. Each one of them has something unique to offer this company and is appreciated in more ways than we can say.

Perhaps the words "heart and soul" stir memories within you in another way. Shelly and I both took piano lessons when we were children. We remember how much fun it was to, once in awhile, take leave of the more mundane parts of practice and break into a carefree duet of "Heart and Soul" with our friends. How much more interesting the music was with four hands, rather than just two...

As you turn through the pages of this book, listen carefully... You may be able to hear us harmonizing from the hills of Lake of the Ozarks.

~ Roxie Kelley

Heart Smart

Misc.

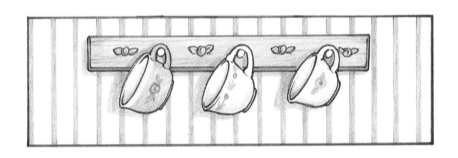

Table of Contents

Appetizers

Breads

Soups and Salads

Main Dishes

Side Dishes

Desserts

Appetizers

SALMON SPREAD

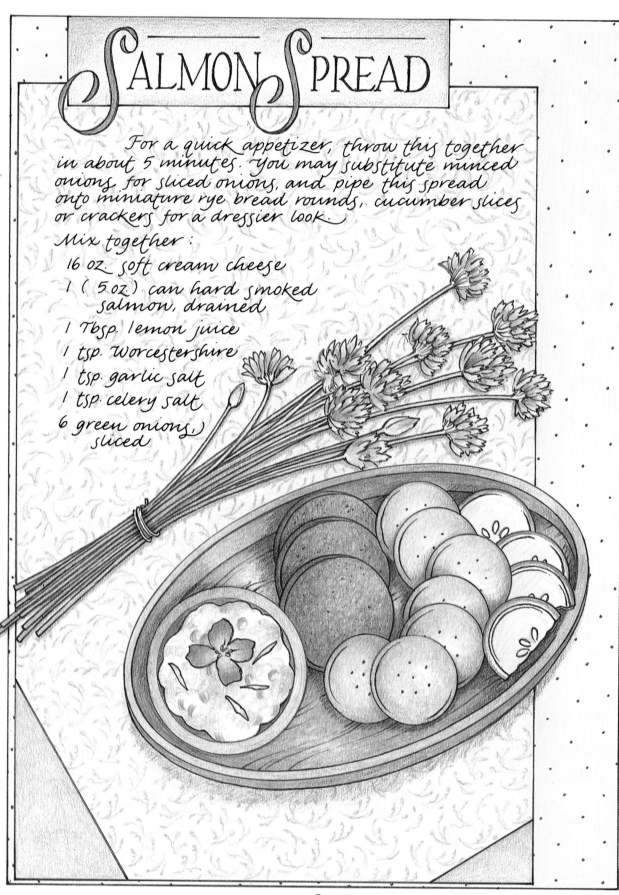

For a quick appetizer, throw this together in about 5 minutes. You may substitute minced onions for sliced onions, and pipe this spread onto miniature rye bread rounds, cucumber slices or crackers for a dressier look.

Mix together:

16 oz. soft cream cheese

1 (5 oz.) can hard smoked salmon, drained

1 Tbsp. lemon juice

1 tsp. Worcestershire

1 tsp. garlic salt

1 tsp. celery salt

6 green onions, sliced

GARLIC Spread

This is a tasty spread that can be prepared with fat-free cream cheese and sour cream as an option to the method described below

Mix together until smooth:
   8 oz. cream cheese, softened
   ¼ cup sour cream

Add:
   2 cloves garlic, crushed
   ¼ tsp. salt
   ¼ cup sliced green onion
      (tops and bottoms)

Serve at room temperature with warm bread. Makes about 10-12 servings. Store leftover spread in an airtight container in the refrigerator.

White Baron
P I Z Z A

Experience the thrill of feasting on a most unusual creation that would excite even "Vern-the-Baron" himself. A special acquaintance and business advisor of the Among Friends girls, this 77-year-old gentleman enjoys two pastimes. You may find him soaring over the Los Angeles airport practicing "grease-landings" or indulging in his favorite menu item, pizza smothered in cheese. Try this recipe and you will land a real winner!

The Crust:

2 cups all-purpose flour	2 tsp. rapid rise yeast
½ cup yellow corn meal	2 Tbsp. olive oil
1 tsp. salt	½ cup warm water
1½ tsp. sugar	¼ cup milk

Heat water and milk in microwave until very warm. Mix dry ingredients. Add water, milk and oil and mix at medium speed with electric mixer for about 2 minutes. Remove from mixer bowl and knead lightly for a few seconds. Form into a ball. Place in a greased bowl and cover lightly with plastic wrap. Let rise in a warm place until doubled (about 30 minutes). *

Remove the dough to a lightly floured surface and knead by hand a few seconds. Then roll out into a 14-inch circle. Place on a pizza stone or pan that has been sprinkled with cornmeal.

* If you wish to speed up the rising of the dough at this point, place a glass with 8 oz. of water in it in the microwave, alongside the bowl with the dough in it. Microwave on defrost setting for 2 minutes. Let rest 3 minutes. Repeat defrost setting for 2 minutes. Let rest 10 minutes.

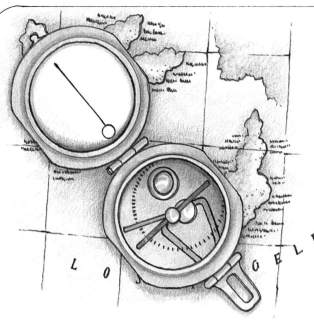

The Sauce:

- 2 Tbsp. butter
- 3 green onions, finely chopped
- 8 oz fresh mushrooms, sliced
- 3/4 cup white wine
- 1 tsp. cornstarch
- 1/2 cup heavy cream
- 1/4 tsp. crushed basil leaves
- 1/2 tsp. parsley

In medium-size frying pan, melt butter. Add green onions and mushrooms and sauté about 1 minute. Add 1/2 cup of wine and boil until liquid is reduced by about half. Shake cornstarch and cream in a tight-fitting, lidded container until cornstarch is dissolved. Add to pan, along with rest of wine and spices. Boil gently until sauce thickens. Remove from heat.

The Toppings:

- 2 cups cooked and diced chicken breast pieces
    (I sauté the chicken in a pan sprayed with vegetable oil, and seasoned lightly with thyme, poultry seasoning and salt.)

- 8-12 oz. mozzarella cheese

- olive oil or butter

- diced tomatoes, or peppers for colors, if desired

Lightly oil or butter the pizza dough. Layer cheese, then sauce, then chicken, then more cheese. Bake immediately at 425° for about 15 minutes. Let cool about 3-4 minutes before slicing.

* Crabmeat and seafood seasoning may be substituted for chicken and poultry seasoning.

JANET'S SAUSAGE STARS

Janet Bartels made these tasty appetizers
for a surprise birthday party for Shelly and me a
few years ago (we are both April birthday girls),
and I have been getting cravings for them ever since.

1 lb. pork sausage
1¼ cup grated cheddar cheese
1¼ cup grated Monterey Jack cheese
1 cup prepared Ranch dressing
1 small can sliced black olives
1 tsp. ground red pepper (or to taste)
1 pkg. Won Ton wrappers

1. Preheat oven to 350°. Cook sausage and drain thoroughly.
2. Combine drained sausage with cheeses, olives, dressing and red pepper.
3. Lightly grease muffin tins.
4. Press one won-ton in each cup and bake 5 minutes.
5. Remove from tins and place on baking sheet. Fill each won-ton with sausage mixture.
6. Bake an additional 5-8 minutes until cheese is bubbly.
Makes 2 dozen.

Dee's Fruit Dip

Dee Stoelting and I have been friends for over 20 years — from our college days on the volleyball court to now, where our lives seem to be interwoven at so many different points. We share many friends in common, which is a real perk for me, because I get to sample her wonderful recipes at gatherings on a regular basis. She has a gift for making even the most ordinary of foods look and taste extraordinary. This is a very simple dip, but it has a way of "dressing up" fruits that are always in season. We usually enjoy it with apple slices, chunks of bananas, pineapple and orange wedges.

8 oz. cream cheese
8 oz. sour cream
7 oz. jar marshmallow creme

Soften cream cheese. Mix together with sour cream and marshmallow cream. Chill until ready to serve.

Most Requested

MEN'S DIP

I don't think you have to be a member of the "He-man Woman Hater's Club" to enjoy this dip. It's just a name, Julie tells me. A special thanks to Julie Gerkowski for sharing this recipe.

8 oz. pkg. cream cheese, softened
8 oz. sour cream
2 pkgs. Italian dressing mix
2 cans tiny or broken shrimp, drained
2 tsp. fresh lemon juice
1 finely chopped green pepper

Mix cream cheese and sour cream together. Add all other ingredients and mix well. Refrigerate until serving time. This tastes best when made a day ahead and flavors are allowed to mix. Serve with chips, crackers or vegetables.

POPPYCOCK

8 cups lightly salted
    popcorn
1 ⅓ cups sugar
1 cup butter
1 tsp. vanilla
½ cup light Karo Syrup
2 cups nuts
    (almonds and pecans
        are best, I think.)

Combine sugar, butter, vanilla and syrup in a saucepan. Cook over medium heat until caramel brown in color, (about 10 minutes after it comes to a boil). While hot, pour over popcorn and nuts, and mix gently. Spread in clusters on a greased cookie sheet.

Mama Candy's NACHOS

Mama Candy was so named because she was famous in our town for being the best "nanny" in the whole county. My children and many more were blessed by her loving care for several years of their pre-school lives. When she tried to retire from "nannyhood", we just couldn't stand the thought of not seeing her every day. So we made her come to work at Among Friends. Thank you, Candy, for this fun recipe (and for so much more).

1 cup chili, canned or homemade

16 oz. can refried beans

1 cup sour cream

1 cup shredded cheddar or Monterrey Jack cheese

1 tsp. onion powder

4 oz. chopped green chiles, drained

Picante sauce

Spread chili in bottom of 9" x 13" glass casserole. Spread refried beans over chili. Mix together sour cream, cheese, onion powder and green chiles and spread over beans. Heat in microwave on high for 3-4 minutes. Cover with picante sauce and serve with corn or tortilla chips.

TEXAS TORTILLA DIP

1 - 8 oz. jar salsa or picante sauce
8 oz. sour cream
1 tsp. dried cilantro
1 tsp. red pepper
3/4 cup baby shrimp, cooked (optional)

Mix all ingredients. Cover and chill.
Serve with tortilla chips.
To reduce fat and calories, substitute
with reduced fat sour cream.

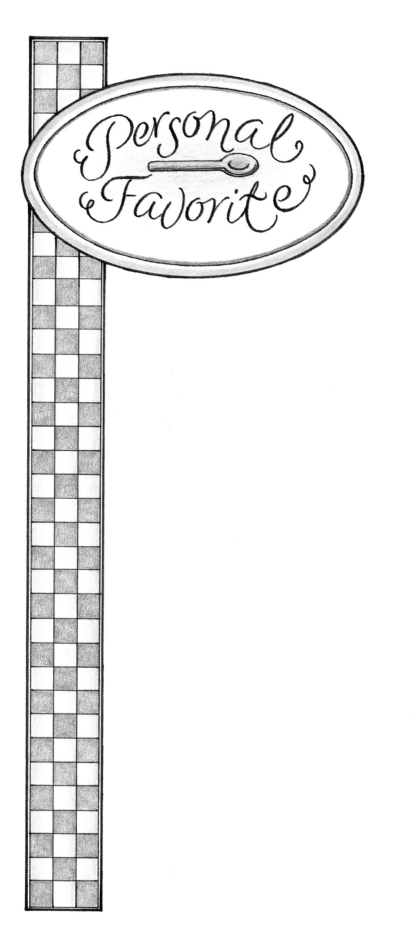

Personal Favorite

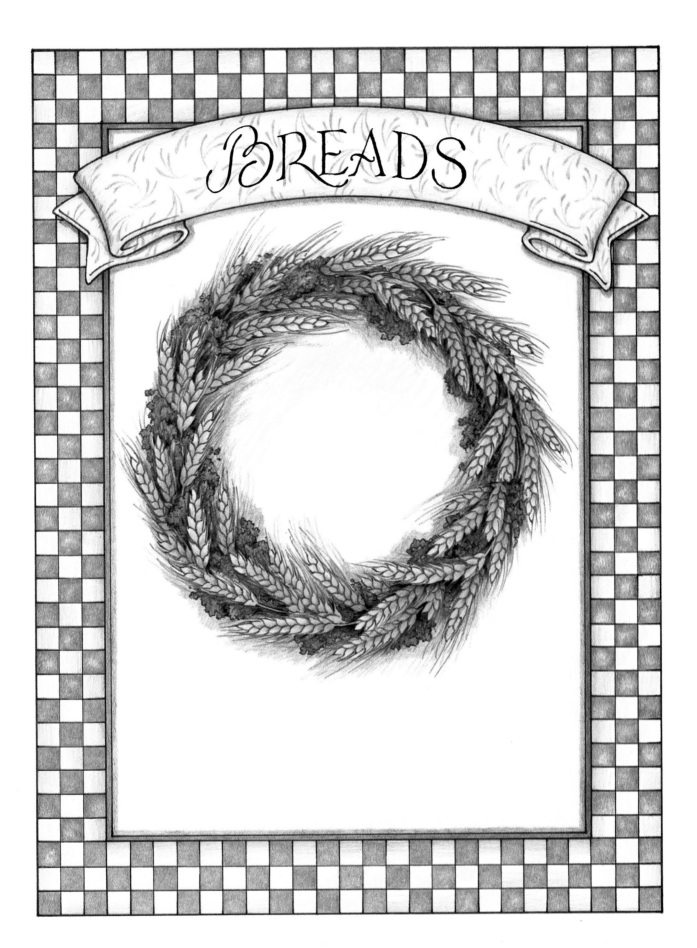

BREADS

BUTTERMILK and CHIVE Biscuits

This biscuit has a wonderful savory flavor that complements any brunch or dinner dish.

♥

2 cups all-purpose flour
1 Tbsp. snipped chives
1 Tbsp. chopped fresh parsley
1 Tbsp. baking powder

1 tsp. sugar
½ tsp. salt
¾ cup buttermilk
¼ cup vegetable oil

3 Tbsp. melted butter

In a medium bowl combine the flour, chives, parsley, baking powder, sugar and salt. Stir in buttermilk and oil all at once. Stir just until blended. Knead lightly about 10 times. Roll out dough onto a lightly floured surface to about ¾" thickness. Cut with floured 2" cutter in a straight down motion, not twisting. Brush bottom of baking pan with melted butter, reserving some for tops of biscuits. Place about 2" apart in pan. Brush tops with remaining butter. Bake in 425° preheated (important) oven for about 15 minutes or until golden. Let cool about 5 minutes before serving.   Makes about 8.

BUNNY MUFFINS

Named after that carrot-loving critter, this muffin has "style and substance". It can be served at an elegant brunch, or tossed into a lunch box. You may omit the raisins and/or nuts if you like.

In a medium-size bowl, blend together:

2 cups flour
2/3 cup brown sugar
1/3 cup sugar

2 tsp. baking soda
1 tsp. baking powder
1 tsp. cinnamon

1/4 tsp. nutmeg

In a separate bowl, combine:

1/2 cup butter, melted
2 eggs, beaten
1/4 cup milk

1 cup shredded carrots
1/2 cup raisins
1/2 cup chopped pecans

Add liquid ingredients to dry and stir until moistened. Spoon into greased muffin cups. Bake in a 350° preheated oven for 18-20 minutes or until golden.
Makes about 1 dozen.

Pumpkin~Cheese Loaves

This is a variation of an earlier recipe from "Just a Matter of Thyme". One of the things I sometimes do to make a nutbread a little extra nice is add a ribbon of cream cheese filling through the middle before it is baked. It works especially well with pumpkin bread, but you may also try this technique with banana or zucchini bread. A word of caution: since you are adding more batter to the pan, you will end up having enough to fill a regular-size loaf pan and a miniature one as well... the perfect gift for a neighbor or friend.

3⅓ cups flour

4 tsp. pumpkin pie spice

2 tsp. baking soda

1 tsp. baking powder

1½ tsp. salt

2⅔ cups sugar

⅔ cups oil

4 eggs

1 lb. can mashed pumpkin

⅔ cup water

1 recipe Cream Cheese Filling (pg. 85)

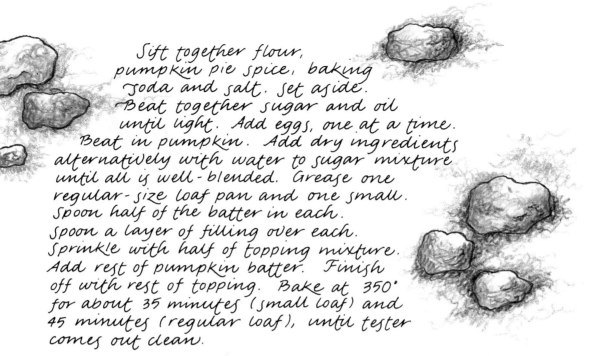

Sift together flour,
pumpkin pie spice, baking
soda and salt. Set aside.
Beat together sugar and oil
until light. Add eggs, one at a time.
Beat in pumpkin. Add dry ingredients
alternatively with water to sugar mixture
until all is well-blended. Grease one
regular-size loaf pan and one small.
Spoon half of the batter in each.
Spoon a layer of filling over each.
Sprinkle with half of topping mixture.
Add rest of pumpkin batter. Finish
off with rest of topping. Bake at 350°
for about 35 minutes (small loaf) and
45 minutes (regular loaf), until tester
comes out clean.

Topping :

2 Tbsp. brown sugar

2 Tbsp. flour

1 tsp. cinnamon

1/4 tsp. pumpkin pie
spice

1 Tbsp. butter

Mix the dry ingredients
together and cut the butter
in until mixture resembles
cornmeal in texture.
Set aside.

Chocolate Banana
MUFFINS

For an interesting addition to the more familiar breakfast or brunch offerings, try try this moist and flavorful muffin.

1¼ cups flour
¾ cup sugar
¼ cup cocoa
1 tsp. baking powder
½ tsp. baking soda
¼ tsp. salt

1 tsp. vanilla
3 ripe bananas, mashed
2 eggs, beaten
2 Tbsp. vegetable oil
2 Tbsp. plain yogurt

Combine first six ingredients in a bowl. Set aside. In a separate bowl, combine bananas and remaining ingredients, add to dry ingredients, stirring just until moistened. Do Not Overmix! Spoon into a greased 12-cup muffin pan, filling two-thirds full.

Mix topping ingredients until crumbly. Sprinkle on top of each muffin pan. Bake in a 400° oven for about 15 min.

Topping

4 large chocolate graham crackers, crushed

½ tsp. ground cinnamon
2 Tbsp. sugar
2 Tbsp. butter

French Bread

This recipe is another example wherein we are reminded that "less is indeed more". How could such simple ingredients produce something so wonderful? Using rapid-rise yeast, you can add this warm bread to any meal with only a two-hour head start.

2 Tbsp. rapid rise yeast
2 Tbsp. sugar
1 Tbsp. salt

2½ cups warm water
7-9 cups flour
1 egg white, beaten

In a large mixing bowl, combine yeast, sugar and salt. Stir in warm water to dissolve. Add 6 cups of the flour. Using the dough hook attachment, mix on high until well blended. Add as much of the remaining flour as needed to make a smooth and elastic dough, kneading about 5 minutes. I add about ¼ cup of flour at a time. Place dough in a greased bowl, turning to coat all sides. Cover and let rise in a warm place until double (about 45-60 minutes). Punch down dough and knead lightly. Shape into two long rolls and place each roll on a greased cookie sheet. Cut shallow slits at 1" intervals along top of bread. Brush with egg white and let rise again until double in size (about 20-30 minutes). Bake 15 minutes in a pre-heated 425° oven. Reduce oven to 350° and continue baking 15 minutes. Cool slightly before cutting to serve.

Anne's BANANA~ OATMEAL Muffins

I am convinced that we have the world's best neighbors in Anne and Dave Wall. No matter how many times I borrow milk or sugar, or how often my children knock on their door, they still love us. It is also handy that both Anne and Dave are excellent cooks ~ we have the most fun gathering our families around one kitchen table or the other. Thanks, Anne, for all the Saturdays you gave up to the "test kitchen".

1 cup rolled oats
1 cup boiling water
3 ripe bananas, mashed
2 eggs, beaten
1 cup sugar
½ cup vegetable oil
1 cup milk
3 cups all-purpose flour
2 ½ tsp. baking soda
½ tsp. salt
1 tsp. cinnamon

Pour water over oats in a bowl and set aside to cool. Mix eggs, sugar, oil, milk and bananas. Stir in cooled oats. Combine flour, baking soda, salt and cinnamon. Add to banana mixture. Bake at 375° for 15-20 minutes. Makes about 18-20 muffins.

20

Jonathon's
APPLESAUCE
Muffins

One of my son's friends, Jonathon Keedy, age 6, ate three of these muffins at a recent gathering... hence, the name.

1 stick butter or margarine	1 tsp. baking soda
1 cup brown sugar	½ tsp. salt
1 egg	1 tsp. cinnamon
2 cups flour	½ tsp. ground cloves
1 tsp. baking powder	1 cup applesauce

½ cup ground pecans

1. Preheat oven to 350° degrees. Spray bottom of the cups of a 12-cup muffin tin with non-stick vegetable oil spray.

2. Cream the butter and the sugar together until smooth. Beat in the egg.

3. In a separate bowl, stir together the flour, baking powder, baking soda, salt, cinnamon and cloves. Mix into the creamed batter.

4. Stir in applesauce and pecans. Spoon the batter into the prepared muffin tins. Bake about 17-20 minutes or until lightly golden.

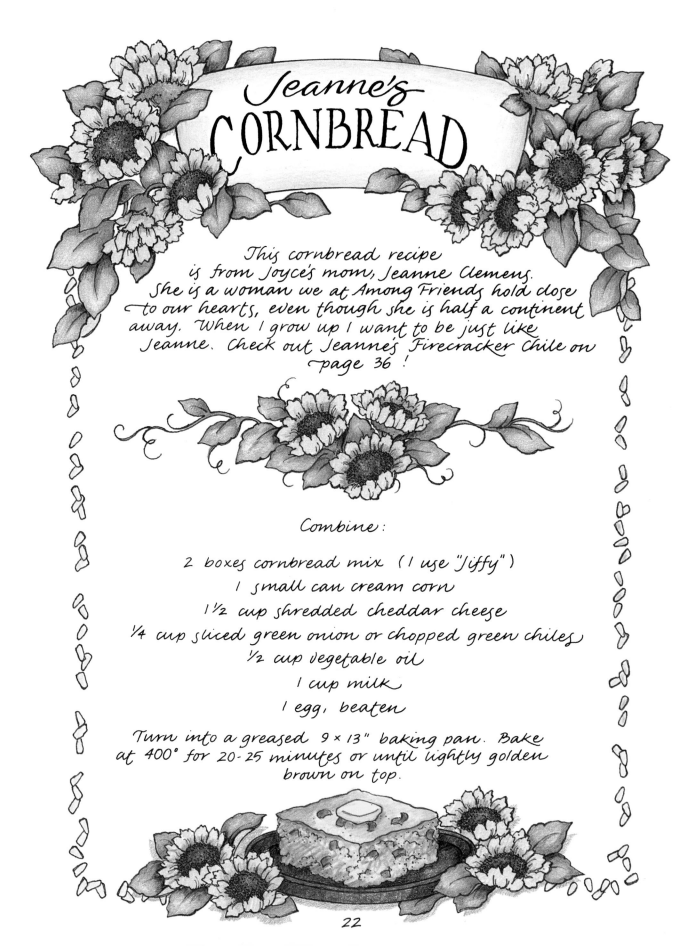

Jeanne's CORNBREAD

This cornbread recipe
is from Joyce's mom, Jeanne Clemens.
She is a woman we at Among Friends hold close
to our hearts, even though she is half a continent
away. When I grow up I want to be just like
Jeanne. Check out Jeanne's Firecracker Chile on
page 36 !

Combine :

2 boxes cornbread mix (I use "Jiffy")

I small can cream corn

1½ cup shredded cheddar cheese

¼ cup sliced green onion or chopped green chiles

½ cup vegetable oil

I cup milk

I egg, beaten

Turn into a greased 9 x 13" baking pan. Bake
at 400° for 20-25 minutes or until lightly golden
brown on top.

Hearty Country Bread

This is a delicious (and good-for-you) bread that can be prepared with only two hours notice. Try it with soup or for sandwiches.

2 Tbsp. rapid rise yeast
1 Tbsp. salt
4 cups whole-wheat flour
3 cups all-purpose flour
½ cup honey
4 Tbsp. margarine or butter
1 egg, room temperature
1 cup quick-cooking oats, uncooked

1. In a large bowl, combine yeast, salt, 2 cups whole-wheat flour and 1 cup all-purpose flour. Heat honey, margarine, and 2¼ cups water until very warm (120° – 130° F). Margarine does not need to melt.

2. With mixer at low speed, gradually beat honey mixture into dry ingredients. Increase speed to medium; beat 2 minutes, scraping bowl occasionally. Beat in egg and 1 cup wheat flour. Continue beating 2 more minutes. Stir in oats, 1 cup whole-wheat flour and 1 cup all-purpose flour.

3. Knead until smooth and elastic, about 10 minutes. You will need to add the rest of the all-purpose flour gradually as you knead. Shape dough into a ball and place in a large, greased bowl, turning dough to grease top. Cover; let rise in warm place until doubled, about 30-45 minutes.

4. Punch down dough. Turn dough onto lightly floured surface and cut in half; cover and let rest 5 minutes. Grease large cookie sheet.

5. Shape each half of dough into oval, tapering ends slightly; place on cookie sheet. Cover; let rise in warm place until doubled, about 30-45 minutes.

6. Preheat oven to 350°. With sharp knife, cut 3 crisscross slashes across top of each loaf. Bake 30-35 minutes until loaves test done. Remove from cookie sheet; cool on wire racks.

Vera's Butterhorns

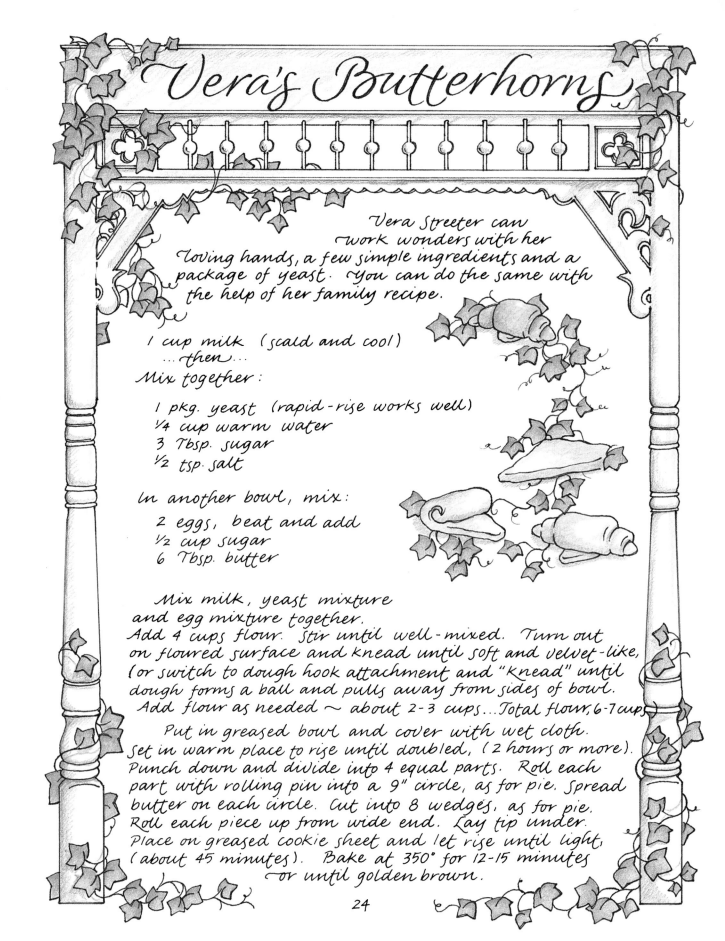

Vera Streeter can work wonders with her loving hands, a few simple ingredients and a package of yeast. You can do the same with the help of her family recipe.

1 cup milk (scald and cool)
  ...then...
Mix together:

    1 pkg. yeast (rapid-rise works well)
    ¼ cup warm water
    3 Tbsp. sugar
    ½ tsp. salt

In another bowl, mix:

    2 eggs, beat and add
    ½ cup sugar
    6 Tbsp. butter

Mix milk, yeast mixture and egg mixture together. Add 4 cups flour. Stir until well-mixed. Turn out on floured surface and knead until soft and velvet-like, (or switch to dough hook attachment and "knead" until dough forms a ball and pulls away from sides of bowl. Add flour as needed ~ about 2-3 cups...Total flour, 6-7 cups.)

Put in greased bowl and cover with wet cloth. Set in warm place to rise until doubled, (2 hours or more). Punch down and divide into 4 equal parts. Roll each part with rolling pin into a 9" circle, as for pie. Spread butter on each circle. Cut into 8 wedges, as for pie. Roll each piece up from wide end. Lay tip under. Place on greased cookie sheet and let rise until light, (about 45 minutes). Bake at 350° for 12-15 minutes or until golden brown.

CINNAMON BUTTER BUNS

This is a "confidence-building" recipe to try if you haven't had much experience baking with yeast. It is relatively quick and easy since you don't "knead" to knead... wonderful served with fresh fruit for breakfast or brunch.

1¼ cup warm water

2 pkgs. dry yeast

¼ cup sugar

1 tsp. salt

½ cup butter or margarine, room temp.

2 eggs, room temp.

3¼ cups flour

1 cup butter or margarine, melted

1 cup sugar, mixed with 2 tsp. cinnamon

Dissolve yeast in warm water to which sugar and salt have been added. Add room temperature butter, eggs and 2 cups of the flour. Beat 2 minutes at medium speed. Add the rest of the flour and beat until smooth. Spoon into 20-24 greased muffin cups (almost half full). Let rise 30-40 minutes. Bake at 375° until golden (about 15-20 minutes). Immediately roll in melted butter and cinnamon/sugar mixture.

25

Cinnamon Breakfast Puffs

1 (11 oz.) package refrigerated soft
breadstick dough
4 Tbsp. butter, melted
3/4 cup sugar
1 Tbsp. cinnamon

Preheat oven to 350°. Spray muffin tin
with a vegetable oil spray. Melt butter in
a shallow bowl. Mix sugar and cinnamon
in another shallow bowl. Open breadstick
dough. The dough should separate into
8 "pinwheels". Unroll each pinwheel, dip
into melted butter, and then into cinnamon
and sugar mixture. Wind back up into
pinwheel again. Place into greased muffin
tin. Repeat with all eight pieces. Bake for
12-14 minutes. Serve while
warm.

Speedy GARLIC CHEESE ROLLS

These dinner rolls are so fast and easy to make, it's embarrassing. Once again, put to use those wonderful refrigerator dough breadsticks ~ with a little T.L.C., in 20 minutes you'll have delicious hot rolls to "pass" with your pasta dish or salad.

1 pkg. refrigerator dough breadsticks (8 in a roll)
2 Tbsp. olive oil
garlic salt
½ cup shredded mild cheddar cheese
1 egg beaten

1. Open package of breadsticks and unroll as if one unit to make a big rectangle. With a pastry brush, lightly spread olive oil evenly over surface of dough. Sprinkle with garlic salt.

2. Sprinkle shredded cheese over surface of dough.

3. One at a time, roll a stick of dough up, pinwheel style, and place into greased muffin tin cup. Repeat for all eight pieces of dough.

4. Brush tops of each roll with beaten egg. Bake at 350° for about 15-18 minutes or until golden brown.

Zach's Stack
Rendezvous Griddlecakes

Zachary Wall's father, Dave, shares his son's favorite pancake recipe with us, in his own words:

1. Mix:

   ½ cup oatmeal
   1½ cups yellow cornmeal
   ¼ cup all-purpose flour
   1 tsp. baking soda
   1 tsp. salt
   1 tsp. sugar

2. Drink some coffee (with brandy and Bailey's Irish cream).*

3. Add:

   1½ cup milk or buttermilk

   2 Tbsp. oil

   1 egg, beaten

4. Drink some more coffee. (Coffee-drinking allows batter to stand a few minutes). Lightly oil a griddle or large skillet and heat over medium heat. Ladle about ¼ cup batter onto griddle, spreading it gently to a 4" round circle. Cook on hot griddle until bubbles form and begin to break on top. Turn pancake over and cook until bottom is golden brown.

   * Author's Note: Sugar and cream may be substituted here without any ill effects to the recipe.

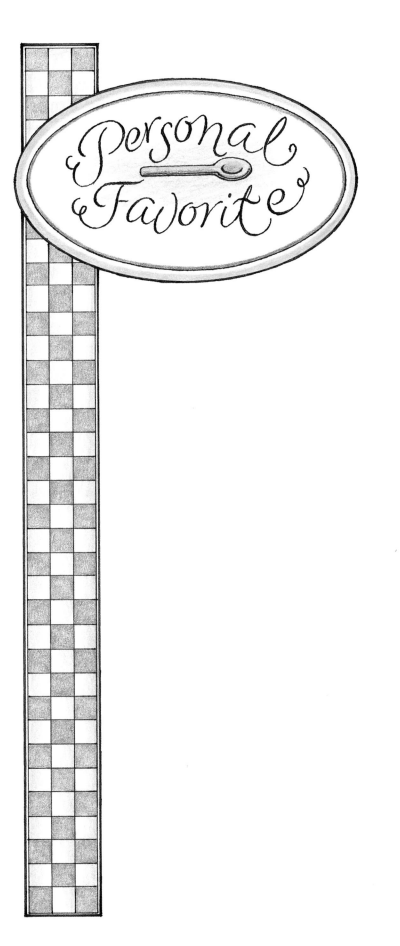

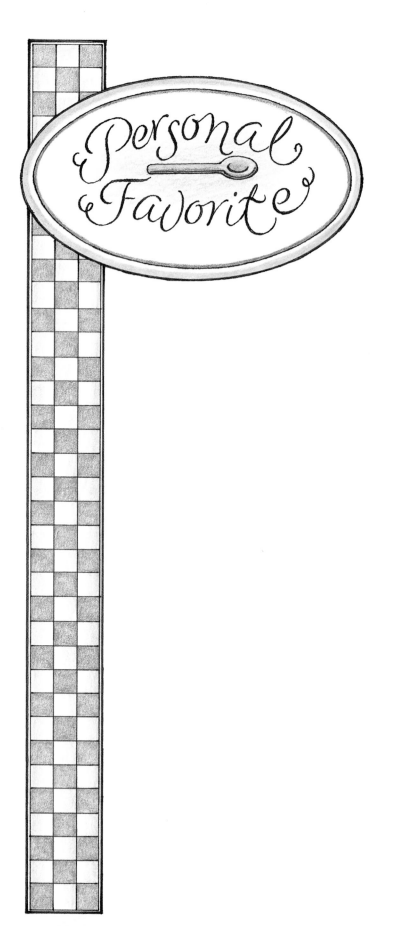

Personal Favorite

Soups and Salads

BAKED STEAK SOUP

When a parent in our community happens to run into Shelley Creed, I suspect they do as I do, and send up a silent prayer of thanks that she is one of our local teachers. She is one of the many over-worked and under-recognized people who make such a big difference in the lives of our children. Besides that, she makes one mean pot of Steak Soup. Stick this in the oven before you send your children off to school... then perhaps write a note of thanks to a favorite teacher...

3 lbs. lean stew meat

3 large carrots, peeled and sliced

8 oz. mushrooms, sliced

1 yellow onion, diced

2 large potatoes, peeled and diced

28 oz. can tomatoes, crushed with juice

10½ oz. can beef consomme

¼ cup white wine (I substituted with water, since Joyce dropped the bottle of wine she was letting me borrow — oops!)

4 Tbsp. tapioca

1 Tbsp. brown sugar

½ cup bread crumbs

1 bay leaf

salt and pepper to taste

peas, canned or frozen, added toward the end of cooking

Mix, cover and put in oven at 250° for at least 6-7 hours.

Note from Roxie: Besides substituting water for wine, you may also substitute the 28 oz. can of tomatoes with a 15 oz. can of salsa-type tomatoes together with a 15 oz. can of chunky tomato sauce (the kind that has onions, celery and bell peppers already mixed in). It's a little spicier than Shelley's recipe, but quite good.

Another Note from Roxie: I have baked this at 300° for about 3½ hours as opposed to the above temperature setting.

33

MEXICAN Confetti STEW

("Kay~bab's Stew")

This quick and spicy dish
was contributed by Kay Routh (affectionately known as
"Kay-bab's" by her loving daughter and son-in-law). A
special thanks to John and Tammy for spending a day in
the "test kitchen" with me and my energetic children,
and for coaxing many fine recipes out of Kay! This one
is especially nice on a fall day with corn muffins and
honey butter.

2 Tbsp. vegetable oil
1 cup chopped onion
1 clove garlic, crushed
2 cups cooked cubed chicken breast
1 can dark red kidney beans, rinsed and drained
2 (14 oz.) cans Mexican or Salsa style stewed tomatoes
1 small package frozen corn
1 can chopped green chiles
1/2 tsp. chili powder
1 tsp. cumin

Saute onion and garlic in oil. Add chicken pieces.
Stir in remaining ingredients. Simmer about 25 minutes.

"MACHO" GAZPACHO

5 cups ripe, peeled tomatoes
1 large clove garlic
2 Tbsp. olive oil
1 Tbsp. wine vinegar
1 tsp. lemon pepper
1 tsp. sugar
½ tsp. salt
1 parsley sprig
4 basil leaves
1 small jar pimentos
2 Tbsp. Italian bread crumbs

Mix all ingredients in a food processor or blender until smooth. Refrigerate at least 8 hours to blend flavors. Serve in chilled bowls with a selection of condiments such as diced cucumber, diced green or yellow pepper, fresh snipped chives, toasted garlic and cheese croutons, and sliced green onions.

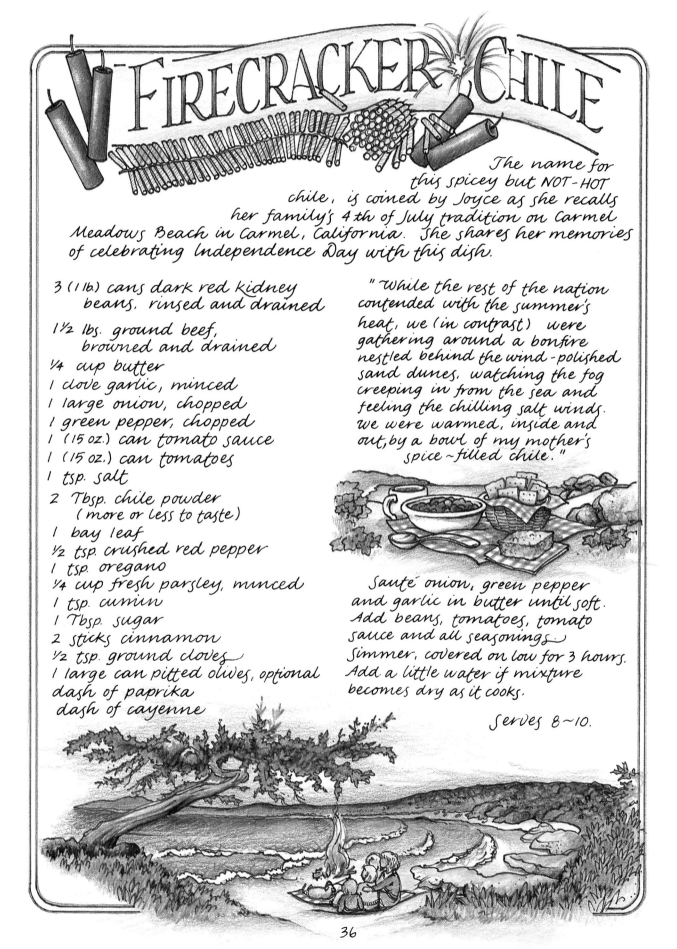

FIRECRACKER CHILE

The name for this spicey but NOT-HOT chile, is coined by Joyce as she recalls her family's 4th of July tradition on Carmel Meadows Beach in Carmel, California. She shares her memories of celebrating Independence Day with this dish.

3 (1 lb.) cans dark red kidney
   beans, rinsed and drained

1½ lbs. ground beef,
   browned and drained

¼ cup butter

1 clove garlic, minced

1 large onion, chopped

1 green pepper, chopped

1 (15 oz.) can tomato sauce

1 (15 oz.) can tomatoes

1 tsp. salt

2 Tbsp. chile powder
   (more or less to taste)

1 bay leaf

½ tsp. crushed red pepper

1 tsp. oregano

¼ cup fresh parsley, minced

1 tsp. cumin

1 Tbsp. sugar

2 sticks cinnamon

½ tsp. ground cloves

1 large can pitted olives, optional

dash of paprika

dash of cayenne

"While the rest of the nation contended with the summer's heat, we (in contrast) were gathering around a bonfire nestled behind the wind-polished sand dunes, watching the fog creeping in from the sea and feeling the chilling salt winds. We were warmed, inside and out, by a bowl of my mother's spice~filled chile."

Sauté onion, green pepper and garlic in butter until soft. Add beans, tomatoes, tomato sauce and all seasonings. Simmer, covered on low for 3 hours. Add a little water if mixture becomes dry as it cooks.

Serves 8~10.

BY THE BAY STEW

This is a wonderful "Cioppino" fish stew that is very easy to make. Try serving it with Hearty Country Bread (page 23). This recipe requires about 45 minutes preparation time.

16 oz. frozen flounder or cod fillets, thawed and cut into bite-size pieces

16 oz. sea scallops, halved
2 Tbsp. vegetable oil
½ green pepper, diced
½ yellow onion, diced

1 garlic clove, minced
28 oz. can tomatoes, crushed
8 oz. bottle of clam juice
¼ cup fresh minced parsley
¼ cup dry sherry
½ tsp. salt
1 tsp. freshly ground pepper

¼ tsp. rubbed sage

In a 5 qt. soup pot over medium heat, cook green pepper, onion and garlic in hot vegetable oil until tender, stirring occasionally. Add tomatoes with their juice, clam juice, parsley, sherry, salt, pepper, sage and fish chunks. Bring heat up to high until mixture boils. Reduce heat to low. Cover and simmer 5 minutes. Add scallops. Cover and simmer 10 minutes longer until fish flakes easily when tested with a fork, and scallops turn opaque.
Makes about 6 main dish servings.

Brooke's Double * Noodle
♥ CHICKEN SOUP ♥

My daughter, Brooke, is a noodle lover. At four years old, it doesn't matter what we have for dinner, as long as there's a noodle in it. Whether your guests are four or 94, I think they will find this soup satisfying. There is nothing like a good chicken soup to take you back to the comforts of home ~ I hope in years to come, the smell of soup cooking in Brooke's kitchen will bring her memories back to me.

In a large stock pot, cover four chicken breasts with water. Cook over medium heat until tender. Remove chicken from broth. Skim fat or strain. Dice chicken into bite-size pieces and return to broth.

♥ Add bouquet garni*,
♥ 2 cups sliced carrots,
♥ 1 yellow onion, diced,
♥ 2 cups sliced celery
♥ 2 (14 oz.) cans chicken broth
♥ 2 tsp. seasoned salt
♥ freshly ground pepper

Cook over medium heat for 45 minutes or until vegetables are tender. Add:

♥ 4 oz. wide egg noodles or "scroodles"
♥ 8 oz. Tortellini

Continue cooking until noodles are tender. Garnish with a generous sprinkling of fresh Parmesan cheese, just to make it interesting.

● ◊ ● ◊ ● ◊ ● ◊ ● ◊ ● ◊ ● ◊ ●

* To make your own bouquet garni, take a piece of cheesecloth (or even a coffee filter) and place 8 peppercorns, 1 bay leaf, 4 sprigs of parsley, and ¼ tsp. dried thyme in the middle. Pull up the edges around the spices to form a little ball. Tie it with some plain white thread. Discard after soup is completely done cooking.

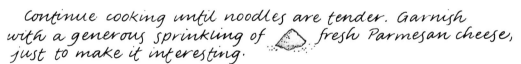

"Until the twelfth of never, I'll still be loving you!" ♪ ♥ ♪ ♩ ♪♪

Cream of Carrot and Tomato Soup

This soup is as beautiful as it is delicious. Served in squash "bowls", as presented here, it is especially festive.

But don't let the lack of availability of squash keep you from preparing this treat.

Using a Dutch oven, sauté leek in butter until limp. Add tomatoes, carrots and salt. Cover and simmer for about 30 minutes. Melt next portion of butter in a sauce pan over low heat. Stir in flour until smooth. Gradually add chicken broth, stirring until mixture has thickened. Combine tomato and broth mixtures in a food processor or blender; process until smooth. Pour into Dutch oven and add milk and whipping cream. Add dill, pepper and tabasco sauce to taste. Meanwhile cut squash in halves, remove seeds, trim small amount from uncut side so that it will set upright. Place cut side down in a small amount of water and microwave 8 minutes until fork tender. Fill cavity with soup, garnish with dollop of sour cream and chopped chives or a sprig of fresh parsley. Note: Enjoy a spoonful of bowl with your soup!

- 1 medium leek, white section sliced
- 2 Tbsp. butter
- 4 cups fresh tomatoes, peeled and chopped
- 1 lb. carrots, peeled and diced
- ½ tsp. salt
- 4 Tbsp. butter
- 4 Tbsp. flour
- 14 ½ oz. can chicken broth
- 2 cups milk
- 1 cup whipping cream
- 2 tsp. dried dill weed, or ¼ cup chopped fresh
- freshly ground pepper
- dash of tabasco sauce
- 1 pint sour cream
- fresh chives or parsley for garnish
- 4 Carnival or Acorn squash (about 12 ounces each)

39

An Herb and a Spice...
Oh so Nice...

Herbs and spices add so much to a recipe if used discriminately and in the right proportions. Overcome your timid tendencies about these flavorings, and invest in an Encyclopedia of Herbs and Spices. It will add a whole new dimension to your cooking.

The herb in this recipe is **Coriander** (the leaf form is known as Cilantro). It is a member of the carrot family and can be found in cuisines around the world. The leaf is sometimes available fresh (but hard to keep) and the seed is found on the grocer's shelf in whole or ground form. Fresh leaves produce the best flavor when chopped and added to the dish at the very last minute. The seeds taste like lemon and sage combined.

The spices in this recipe are **Cumin** and **Chili Powder**.

Cumin should be used sparingly because it tends to dominate among the spices. It is similar in appearance to caraway seed, and has a pungent and slightly bitter flavor.

Chili Powder is a seasoning blend, which consists of relatively mild chili peppers (dried and crushed in a spice grinder), oregano, cumin, garlic and salt. The heat and spiciness can vary depending on the blend.

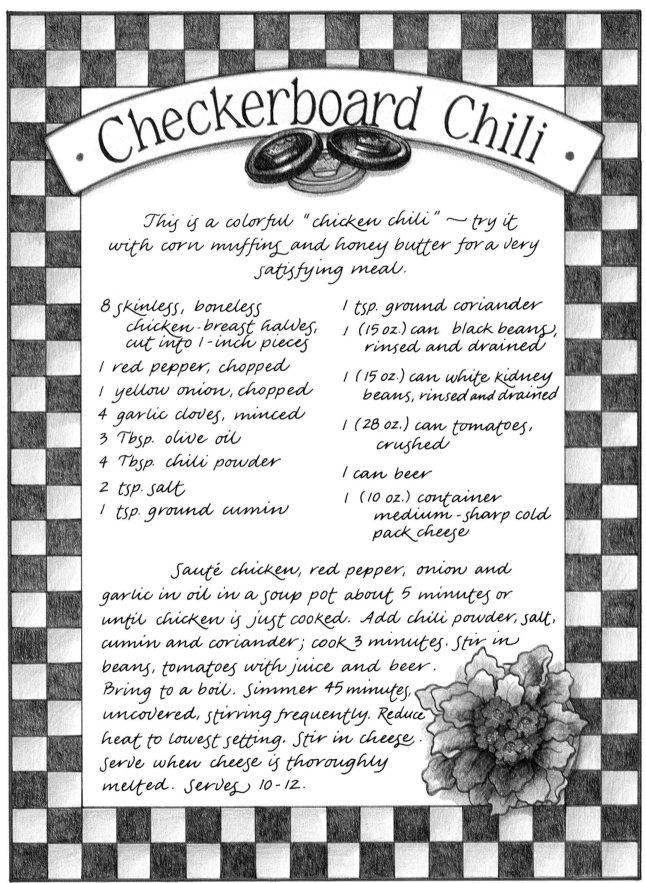

· Checkerboard Chili ·

This is a colorful "chicken chili" ~ try it with corn muffins and honey butter for a very satisfying meal.

8 skinless, boneless chicken-breast halves, cut into 1-inch pieces
1 red pepper, chopped
1 yellow onion, chopped
4 garlic cloves, minced
3 Tbsp. olive oil
4 Tbsp. chili powder
2 tsp. salt
1 tsp. ground cumin

1 tsp. ground coriander
1 (15 oz.) can black beans, rinsed and drained
1 (15 oz.) can white kidney beans, rinsed and drained
1 (28 oz.) can tomatoes, crushed
1 can beer
1 (10 oz.) container medium-sharp cold pack cheese

Sauté chicken, red pepper, onion and garlic in oil in a soup pot about 5 minutes or until chicken is just cooked. Add chili powder, salt, cumin and coriander; cook 3 minutes. Stir in beans, tomatoes with juice and beer. Bring to a boil. Simmer 45 minutes, uncovered, stirring frequently. Reduce heat to lowest setting. Stir in cheese. Serve when cheese is thoroughly melted. Serves 10-12.

North Shore
Chicken Salad

This lively rendition of the "classic" chicken salad was contributed by Judy Goplerud, owner of Home Sweet Home and The Cottage Sampler Tea Room in St. Ansgar, Iowa.

Dressing

2 large cloves garlic, minced
1 Tbsp. Dijon mustard
½ tsp. salt
¼ tsp. sugar
¼ tsp. fresh ground pepper
¼ cup rice wine vinegar
⅓ cup vegetable oil

Salad

4 cups cooked long grain and
    wild rice (cooked in chicken stock)

1 chicken breast (whole), cooked and
    cubed

3 green onions, including tops, sliced

½ red pepper, diced

2 oz. pea pods, cut into 1" pieces

1-2 ripe avocados, cut into medium-
    size pieces

1 cup toasted pecan halves
    lettuce leaves

Dressing: Combine all ingredients
in food processor, blend thoroughly. (or mix
all ingredients together well in a bowl.)

Salad: Toss warm rice in a medium bowl. Cool.
Add chicken, onions, red pepper and
pea pods, toss with dressing. Cover.
Refrigerate 2 to 4 hours. Just before serving
add avocados and pecans. Toss gently.
Transfer to salad bowl. Garnish with
lettuce leaves.

BISTRO TUNA SALAD

As much as I love the traditional tuna salad my mom taught me to make thirty years ago, this certainly is a refreshing option... I like to serve it with the same dressing used in the Spring Potato Salad (page 49). It is especially fun to serve because nearly all the ingredients can be prepared the day before and tossed together at the last moment:

- ♥ I can water-packed tuna, drained
- ♥ ½ lb. fresh green beans
- ♥ 5 small red potatoes
- ♥ I pint cherry tomatoes ~ remove stem and rinse
- ♥ 2 eggs, hard cooked, peeled and quartered
- ♥ I head red leaf lettuce ~ washed and gently dried
- ♥ I head iceberg lettuce ~ washed and gently dried

Spring Potato Salad Dressing

Wash green beans and trim off ends. Place in sauce pan and cover with water. Bring to a boil and cook for about 2 minutes. Drain immediately and rinse with cold water for I minute. Scrub potatoes and slice ½" thick. Cook in salted water until just tender. Drain and cool. Just before serving, toss remaining ingredients together with dressing. Yummy!

Note from Roxie: You may substitute chicken breast, turkey or ham for the tuna if you wish.

RASPBERRY PECAN Salad

This salad is best if you can prepare the dressing ahead of time and chill for several hours. Combine the first 5 ingredients a few minutes before serving and toss gently. This is such a beautiful salad ~ I like to serve the rose-colored dressing in a glass bowl on the side, followed by a small basket of croutons. Serves 10-12.

- ♥ 6 cups torn Boston lettuce
- ♥ 6 cups torn Red Leaf lettuce
- ♥ ½ cup pecan pieces
- ♥ Raspberry Salad Dressing
- ♥ 1 cup fresh or frozen raspberries
- ♥ 1 avacado, peeled and cubed.
- ♥ Croutons

RASPBERRY Dressing

⅓ cup seedless raspberry jam

⅓ cup raspberry vinegar

1 cup vegetable oil

1 Tbsp. poppy seeds

Combine jam and vinegar in a blender or food processor and blend for 15-20 seconds.

With blender on high, gradually add oil in a slow, steady stream. Stir in poppy seeds. Chill well before serving.

Lori's GREEK SALAD

At a recent visit to Ann's house (my true blue friend from South Carolina), we enjoyed this light and tangy salad. She acquired the recipe from Lori and I honestly don't know who gave it to Lori. Sometimes it's difficult to get to the bottom of these things. However, we easily found the bottom of this bowl.

1 head Romaine lettuce
1 red pepper
1 purple onion
2-3 cucumbers
2-3 tomatoes
1 small can black olives, drained
½ jar pepperoncini
1 oz. pkg. feta cheese (crumbly type)

Dressing:

scant ½ cup pepperoncini juice
dash red wine vinegar
dash olive oil

salt and pepper to taste
dried basil to taste
(try ½ tsp.)

1. Clean lettuce. Spin dry and tear into small pieces. Put into a paper towel-lined bowl in the refrigerator while preparing other vegetables and dressing.

2. Cut pepper and onion into slices. Peel and dice cucumbers. Cut tomatoes into 1" chunks.

3. Wisk together all dressing ingredients.

4. Toss all of the vegetables with lettuce, including olives and pepperoncini. Top with cheese and dressing. Toss well. Return to refrigerator until ready to serve.

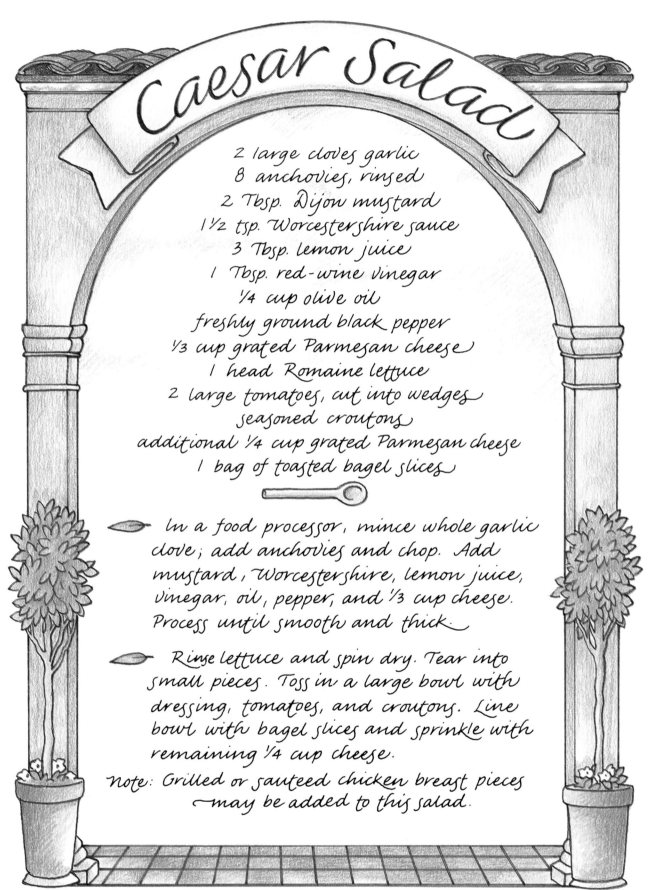

Caesar Salad

2 large cloves garlic
8 anchovies, rinsed
2 Tbsp. Dijon mustard
1½ tsp. Worcestershire sauce
3 Tbsp. lemon juice
1 Tbsp. red-wine vinegar
¼ cup olive oil
freshly ground black pepper
⅓ cup grated Parmesan cheese
1 head Romaine lettuce
2 large tomatoes, cut into wedges
seasoned croutons
additional ¼ cup grated Parmesan cheese
1 bag of toasted bagel slices

In a food processor, mince whole garlic clove; add anchovies and chop. Add mustard, Worcestershire, lemon juice, vinegar, oil, pepper, and ⅓ cup cheese. Process until smooth and thick.

Rinse lettuce and spin dry. Tear into small pieces. Toss in a large bowl with dressing, tomatoes, and croutons. Line bowl with bagel slices and sprinkle with remaining ¼ cup cheese.

Note: Grilled or sauteed chicken breast pieces may be added to this salad.

47

Jan's Fruit Salad

Without getting too sentimental, let me just say that I have a great sister. (You know Jan, of "Jan's Brownie" fame in "Just a Matter of Thyme".) It is true God gives us lots of friends, but He gives us only a very small number of actual "soul mates" in life. I am so very grateful she is one of mine.

Prepare any combination of the following fruits, cutting up into bite-size pieces.

1 fresh pineapple
2 kiwis
1 cantaloupe

1 papaya
strawberries, halved
green grapes

Use Your Imagination Here!

Dressing:

Combine in a blender:

2 ripe bananas
1 cup sour cream
4 Tbsp. brown sugar
1½ tsp. lemon juice

Pour dressing over fruit and... Enjoy!

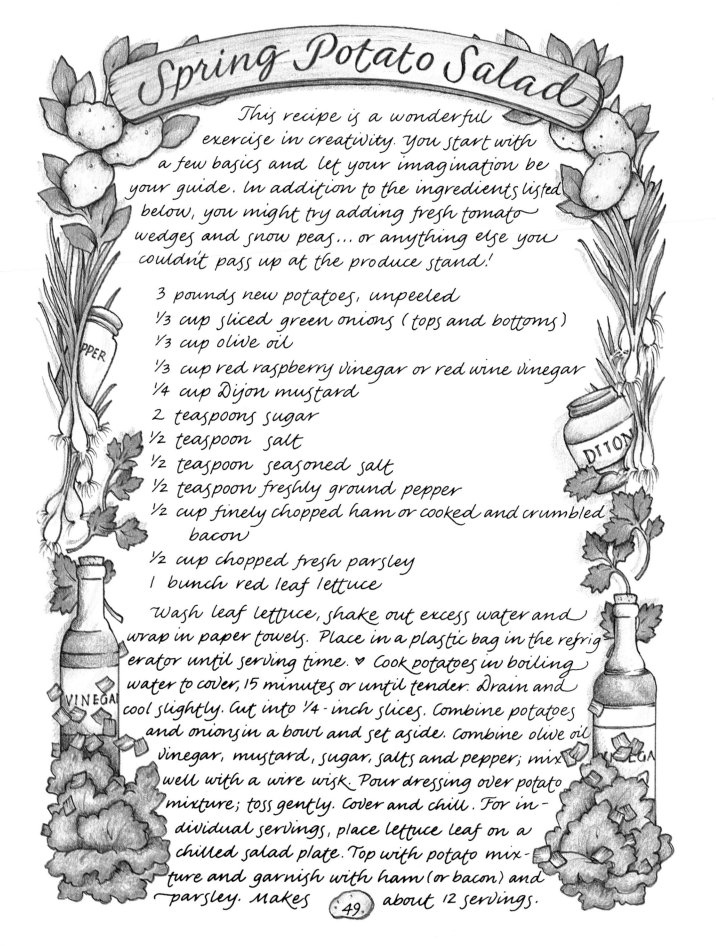

Spring Potato Salad

This recipe is a wonderful exercise in creativity. You start with a few basics and let your imagination be your guide. In addition to the ingredients listed below, you might try adding fresh tomato wedges and snow peas... or anything else you couldn't pass up at the produce stand!

3 pounds new potatoes, unpeeled
1/3 cup sliced green onions (tops and bottoms)
1/3 cup olive oil
1/3 cup red raspberry vinegar or red wine vinegar
1/4 cup Dijon mustard
2 teaspoons sugar
1/2 teaspoon salt
1/2 teaspoon seasoned salt
1/2 teaspoon freshly ground pepper
1/2 cup finely chopped ham or cooked and crumbled bacon
1/2 cup chopped fresh parsley
1 bunch red leaf lettuce

Wash leaf lettuce, shake out excess water and wrap in paper towels. Place in a plastic bag in the refrigerator until serving time. ♥ Cook potatoes in boiling water to cover, 15 minutes or until tender. Drain and cool slightly. Cut into 1/4-inch slices. Combine potatoes and onions in a bowl and set aside. Combine olive oil, vinegar, mustard, sugar, salts and pepper; mix well with a wire wisk. Pour dressing over potato mixture; toss gently. Cover and chill. For individual servings, place lettuce leaf on a chilled salad plate. Top with potato mixture and garnish with ham (or bacon) and parsley. Makes about 12 servings.

49

TURBO SLAW

Rebecca Flynn
"is one of the most energetic, positive people
I have ever had the pleasure to meet. She is usually
"on the move", so we actually had to hold her captive
in my kitchen one afternoon to get her to stand still
long enough to write out this recipe. Becky has
earned the title of our Best Sales Rep of the Year
for two years running, so we are NOT complaining
about her active lifestyle.

This family favorite was once served
in a huge tub at Becky's husband's sister's wedding
(did you get all that?) Her father-in-law thought
he heard Becky ask someone to get the "turbo slaw"
(tub of slaw). The name just stuck.

A TUB O' SLAW

1 head of cabbage, shredded
2 pkgs. Ramen noodles, uncooked and crumbled
spice packet from noodle package
1 Tbsp. sesame seeds or poppy seeds
2 tsp. celery salt
½ cup chopped celery
½ cup shredded carrots
½ cup chopped cauliflower
8 oz. bottle oil and red wine vinegar dressing

Toss all ingredients. Refrigerate for at least 3 hours.

Note from Roxie: Just for fun, we sprinkled some
soy sauce into this dish, too. You might try it
both ways.

50

GRANDMA ADAMEC'S Broccoli Slaw

1 bunch fresh broccoli, broken into small pieces
½ lb. bacon, cooked and crumbled
½ cup diced red onion
2 Tbsp. sesame seeds
¼ cup raisins

Dressing

1 cup mayonnaise
2 Tbsp. vinegar
¼ cup sugar

Combine all vegetables, seeds and raisins in a medium-size serving bowl. Pour dressing over vegetables and refrigerate until ready to serve.

Serves 6-8.

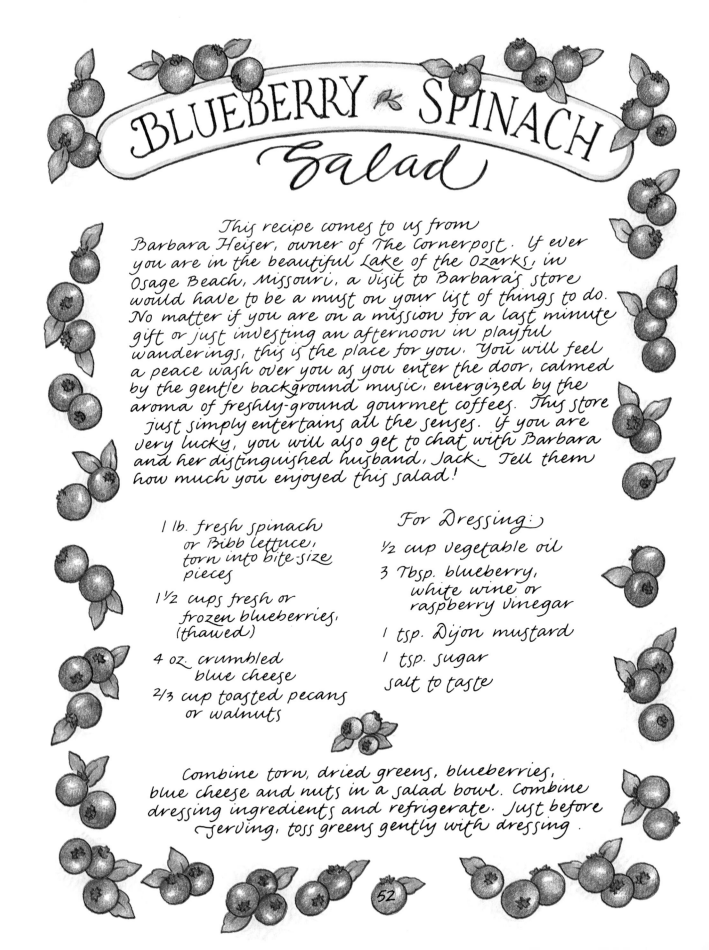

BLUEBERRY & SPINACH Salad

This recipe comes to us from Barbara Heiser, owner of The Cornerpost. If ever you are in the beautiful Lake of the Ozarks, in Osage Beach, Missouri, a visit to Barbara's store would have to be a must on your list of things to do. No matter if you are on a mission for a last minute gift or just investing an afternoon in playful wanderings, this is the place for you. You will feel a peace wash over you as you enter the door, calmed by the gentle background music, energized by the aroma of freshly-ground gourmet coffees. This store just simply entertains all the senses. If you are very lucky, you will also get to chat with Barbara and her distinguished husband, Jack. Tell them how much you enjoyed this salad!

1 lb. fresh spinach or Bibb lettuce, torn into bite-size pieces

1½ cups fresh or frozen blueberries, (thawed)

4 oz. crumbled blue cheese

2/3 cup toasted pecans or walnuts

For Dressing:

½ cup vegetable oil

3 Tbsp. blueberry, white wine or raspberry vinegar

1 tsp. Dijon mustard

1 tsp. sugar

salt to taste

Combine torn, dried greens, blueberries, blue cheese and nuts in a salad bowl. Combine dressing ingredients and refrigerate. Just before serving, toss greens gently with dressing.

The Scoop on the Soup

Ever wonder what distinguishes broth from bouillon? Consommé from stock? Maybe these definitions will help...

Broth is made by simmering meat, poultry or fish in water, often with vegetables and herbs. The fat is removed once the cooking is complete, and the liquid is strained.

Bouillon is clear, seasoned broth.

Stock is a richly flavored broth with meat and/or vegetables.

Consommé is a clear, strong broth made of one or more kinds of meat plus some vegetables. It is cooked down, so that it has half the volume and twice the flavor of broth. Well seasoned and strained, it is served either as a hot soup or a cold jelly.

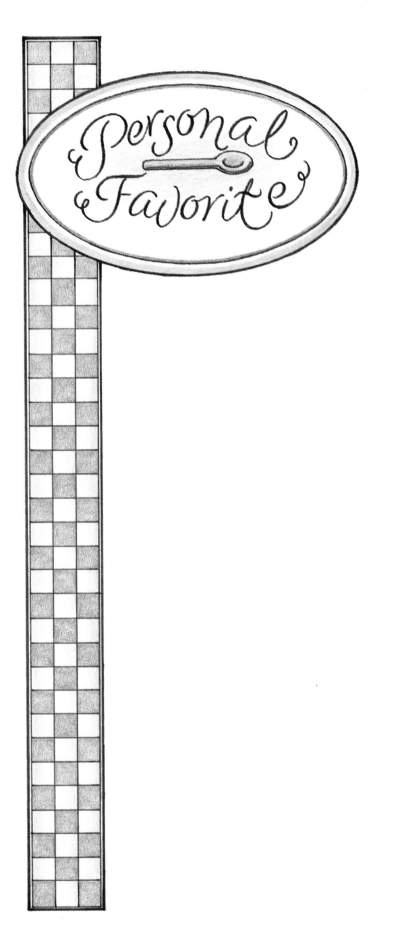

Personal Favorite

MAIN DISHES

Calico Shops

ESCALLOPED CHICKEN

Our thanks to Ramona Birdsell, owner of Calico Shops and Thymes Remembered Tea Room for this elegant chicken creation.

1 loaf cubed white bread
4 cups diced cooked chicken
1 cup diced celery
¼ cup minced onion
1½ cups salad dressing

1 can sliced water chestnuts
4 eggs
3 cups milk
2 cans cream of chicken soup
¾ cup mayonnaise

salt, pepper, grated cheddar cheese, sliced almonds

Spray 9" x 12" pan with non-stick spray. Place ½ of bread on bottom of pan. Mix together chicken, celery, onion, salad dressing and water chestnuts. Place on top of bread, then top with remainder of bread cubes. Mix together eggs, milk, salt and pepper and pour over all. Cover and let stand overnight in refrigerator.

Bake covered about 1 hour. Remove cover. Mix together soup and mayo and spread on top of chicken dish. Sprinkle cheese and almonds on top. Bake uncovered about 15 minutes. Serves 12-15 people.

SPINACH PIE

This savory pie is wonderful as a main dish anytime of year. Serve with buttery carrots on the side and enjoy...

♥ 1 recipe for double crust pie (or 1 pkg. refrigerator type)

♥ 2 Tbsp. butter

♥ 3 cups shredded zucchini

♥ 8 oz. fresh mushrooms, sliced

♥ 1 tsp. seasoned salt

♥ 1 pkg. (10 oz.) frozen spinach, thawed and squeezed dry

♥ 15 oz. ricotta cheese

♥ 8 oz. french cream cheese, softened *

♥ 1 cup shredded mozzarella cheese

♥ 2 large eggs, lightly beaten

♥ 1 Tbsp. Tabasco

♥ 1 egg, beaten with 1 Tsp. water

Prepare pie crusts and set aside. Melt butter in skillet over medium-high heat and add zucchini and mushrooms. Sprinkle with seasoned salt and cook until just tender. Remove from heat. Combine spinach, ricotta, cream cheese, mozzarella, eggs and Tabasco in large bowl. Stir in zucchini and mushrooms. Line pie plate or baking dish with one pie crust. Spoon in filling. Top with second pie crust. Cut vents in top and flute edges. Brush with egg glaze. Bake at 425° for 15 minutes, then at 375° for 35-45 minutes more until golden. Cool on wire rack for 30 minutes.

10 servings

* See "Boursin Cheese" in Just a Matter of Thyme, or look for cream cheese with herbs and garlic in the grocery's dairy case.

Kelly's Folly

WICKERLEIGH'S PORCH EGGS BENEDICT ♥

Marc and Kelly Barnett have a little "family tradition". Whenever they are on vacation, they make a special point to find the best Eggs Benedict around to satisfy Kelly's craving. We had no choice but to name our house specialty after Kelly.

♦ ♦ ♦

6 egg yolks	8 slices Canadian bacon
3 oz. cream cheese	8 poached eggs
1 cup butter	chives or parsley for garnish
dash cayenne pepper	paprika
1½ Tbsp. fresh lemon juice	4 whole English muffins

Place egg yolks, cream cheese and dash of cayenne pepper in blender. Blend until smooth. Melt butter in microwave until butter is very hot, being careful not to burn. Slowly pour butter over egg mixture while blender is on low speed. Add lemon juice. Continue to mix until thick and smooth, about 30 seconds. Should sauce become too thick, simply add a small amount of hot water. Split English muffins with fork, toast lightly. Warm Canadian bacon in either microwave or skillet. Gently poach eggs.

Place a slice of bacon on top of each muffin, then a poached egg. Drizzle sauce over top, sprinkle with paprika and fresh chives or parsley. Serves 4.

Note: For a wonderful low-fat alternative to this dish, check our Heart Smart section for "Love Your Heart", another fun menu item from Wickerleigh's Porch.

Hash QUICHE Brown

3 cups loose-pack frozen hash-
 brown potatoes, thawed
⅓ cup butter, melted
6-8 oz. diced, cooked ham
¼ cup chopped tomatoes
¼ cup sliced green onions
8 oz. mild cheddar cheese, shredded
½ cup milk or Half n Half
3 eggs
¼ tsp. seasoned salt
½ tsp. tarragon

1. Press hash browns between paper towels to
   remove moisture. Then press onto bottom and
   up sides of a 9" pie plate to form a crust.

2. Drizzle melted butter over crust. Bake in
   425° oven for 25 minutes. Remove from oven.
   Reduce oven temperature to 350°.

3. In a bowl, toss together ham, cheese, tomatoes
   and onion. Place ham mixture in crust.
   Beat together milk, eggs and seasonings.
   Pour milk mixture over ham mixture.

4. Bake, uncovered, in the 350° oven for 25-30
   minutes. Let stand for 10 minutes before serving.

Makes 6 servings

SHRIMP CREOLE

For a period of time, Joyce and her husband, Del, lived in Mississippi. It was there that they became acquainted with their neighbors, The Hiltons, and not too long after that ~ they fell in love with Teency Hilton's Shrimp Creole. When I asked Joyce and Del to describe Teency, they simply said she was just like her name, tiny and classy. Teency is gone now, but I'm sure her husband, Jimmy, is pleased to know that people everywhere are enjoying this dish.

2 onions, chopped
1 clove garlic, minced
1 bell pepper, finely chopped
1 cup finely chopped celery
4 Tbsp. butter
2 (8 oz.) cans tomato sauce
1 cup water
1 tsp. beef bouillon
2 bay leaves

3/4 tsp. salt
2 tsp. chopped parsley
1/8 tsp. cayenne pepper
pinch of soda
pinch of sugar
1 Tbsp. pickapepper sauce
juice of one lemon
1/2 tsp. mace
dash of black pepper

about 75 shrimp, peeled and deveined
enough rice for six servings, prepared according to package directions

Sauté onion, garlic, green pepper and celery in butter. Stir in tomato sauce, water and seasonings. Simmer 20-30 minutes. Stir in shrimp; simmer gently until shrimp are tender. Serve over rice.

CHICKEN JAMBALAYA

Another great dish from Joyce's kitchen!

2 whole chicken breasts

2 quarts water

bouquet garni

1 lb. smoked sausage, sliced, browned and drained

1 large green pepper, chopped

1 onion, chopped

2 ribs celery, chopped

4 cloves garlic, minced

2 bunches green onions, chopped

½ cup butter or margarine

2½ cups long grain rice

♥

3 chicken bouillon cubes

½ tsp. Tabasco

1½ tsp. Worcestershire sauce

1 Tbsp. Kitchen Bouquet

Simmer chicken in water with bouquet garni, until tender (about 45 min.). Debone and cut chicken into chunks. Reserve the stock. In a large Dutch oven, sauté the vegetables in butter until soft. Add sausage, 6 cups of the stock, rice and seasonings. Cover and simmer over low heat 45-60 minutes adding more stock if necessary. During last 5 minutes, gently stir in chicken.

Note from Joyce: The name Jambalaya originated from the Spanish word, "jamon" (ham), but is said to be a colloquialism for "clean up the kitchen". Ham or shrimp may be the major ingredients but various combinations of sausage, chicken, game, oysters, crabmeat, and other kinds of meat or fish may be used.

Brisket

Sometimes I put this dish together in the slow cooker before I leave for work. The wonderful aroma drifts from the kitchen to greet me as I return home ~ it's one of those moments when life doesn't seem so difficult.

Mix and set aside ½ cup:

3/4 cup water
1/4 cup Worcestershire sauce
1 Tbsp. wine vinegar
1 tsp. chile powder
½ tsp. dry mustard
pinch of ground red pepper
2 cloves garlic, minced

♥   ♥   ♥

After reserving ½ cup of the above mixture, pour remaining over 2½ lbs. of fresh beef brisket in a 4-quart crockery cooker. Cook on low for about 10 hours, or on high for 4-5 hours. When ready to serve, remove the meat from the cooker and discard cooking liquid.

Make barbeque sauce using reserved liquid from above, adding:

½ cup catsup
2 Tbsp. brown sugar
1 tsp. cornstarch

Stir over medium high heat until thickened and bubbly. Stir an additional 2 minutes. Slice meat diagonally across the grain and serve on warm rolls. Pass the sauce.

Blake's FISH D·I·S·H

My son, Blake, probably came to love fish at such an early age because of "Grandpa Jack". Jack and Marie (Blake's babysitter) lived on the lake, and together they taught Blake from age 9 months on about water safety and respecting Mother Nature. I am grateful for the memory I have etched in my heart of the three of them, sitting on the dock with their life jackets on, learning from each other about life and love. There are lots of moments when I am especially proud of Blake and his thoughtful ways, and I know I owe so much of his sweet disposition to this couple...

This is a very simple dish to prepare. Perhaps you could spend a few minutes in the kitchen with your son, if you are blessed enough to have one, and enlist his help!

1 lb. fish fillets
½ cup melted butter
seasoned salt to taste
lemon pepper to taste
1 lemon, cut into wedges

Wash and dry fish and place in a shallow, foil-lined pan. Brush melted butter over fish and season. Bake at 400° for about 15-20 minutes or until fish flakes easily with a fork. Squeeze lemon juice over fish right before serving or garnish with wedges. Serving suggestions: Especially nice with sautéed mushrooms, wild rice or noodles, and peas.

"The Spicery" CHICKEN & RICE

Donna Kidwell from "The Spicery Tea Room" in Tuscola, Illinois, says this is a favorite of her customers. The recipe is from her mother's collection.

1 cup wild rice
1/2 cup chopped onion
1/2 cup butter
1/4 cup flour
6 oz. can broiled, sliced
    mushrooms
1 1/2 cups chicken broth

1 1/2 cups light cream
3 cups diced cooked chicken
    (5 breasts)
1/4 cup diced pimento
2 Tbsp. parsley
1 1/2 tsp. salt
1/4 tsp. pepper

1/2 cup slivered blanched almonds

Prepare wild rice according to package directions. Cook onion in butter until tender but not brown. Remove from heat; stir in flour. Drain mushrooms, reserving liquid. Add chicken broth and stir into flour mixture. Add cream. Cook and stir until thick. Add rice, mushrooms, chicken, pimento, parsley, salt and pepper. Place in a 2 qt. casserole. Sprinkle with almonds. Bake in 350° oven 25-30 minutes.

Turkey Forestier

This recipe is from Suzanne Feeney, owner of "Impressions by Suzanne" a ten-year-old business nestled in historic Roswell, Georgia.

6 Turkey Cutlets
2 Tbsp. olive oil
3 Tbsp. flour
¼ tsp. each, salt and pepper
8 oz. fresh mushrooms
¼ cup white vermouth
juice of a fresh lemon

Pound the turkey cutlets between two pieces of wax paper Dredge in flour, salt and pepper mixture. Heat olive oil in non-stick pan and brown the cutlets. Remove from pan and keep warm. Add mushrooms and cook 3 minutes. Add vermouth to deglaze pan. Put meat back in pan to warm.
Sprinkle with lemon juice before serving.

Serves 4-6.

Julie's
SWEET & SOUR
B E E F

Another recipe from one of the "Ebert" girls in our office ~ and another wonderful option when you are looking for something you can put in ~ ~ the slow cooker.

- 2# round steak or stew meat, cut in 1" cubes
- 2 Tbsp. vegetable oil
- 16 oz. tomato sauce
- 2 tsp. chile powder
- 2 tsp. paprika
- ¼ cup sugar
- 1 tsp. salt
- ½ cup vinegar
- ½ cup light molasses or syrup
- 2 cups sliced carrots
- 2 cups small white onions
- 1 green pepper, sliced
- enough cooked rice for 4-6 servings

Brown meat in oil. Put in slow cooker. Add all remaining ingredients and mix. Cook 6-7 hours on low or 4 hours on high. Serve over rice.

66

DEEP DISH Steak Pie

1 box refrigerator pie crust
   dough (or your favorite
   homemade version)
1 ½ lb. boneless beef sirloin
   or stew meat
2 Tbsp. vegetable oil
½ cup beef broth
¼ cup white wine
1 clove garlic, minced
1 tsp. dried marjoram, crushed
salt and pepper to taste

1 bay leaf
3 Tbsp. butter
2 potatoes, peeled and
   thinly sliced
2 carrots, thinly sliced
1 onion, peeled and
   chopped
⅓ cup flour
1 cup half and half
1 cup frozen peas
1 egg, beaten

Prepare pie crust. Set aside. Brown meat in oil.
Stir in broth, wine, garlic and seasonings. Bring to a boil.
Reduce heat; simmer, covered, 10 minutes. In a large
saucepan, melt butter. Add potatoes, carrots, onion and
cook until tender, but not brown. Stir in flour. Add half
and half; cook and stir until thickened and bubbly. Stir
in the meat mixture; add the peas. Heat through.
Transfer mixture to a 2 qt. casserole; place pie crust on top.
Prick with a fork several times. Turn pastry edge under and
press gently to make it stick to the edge of the casserole dish.
Brush with beaten egg. Bake at 400° for about 30 minutes
or until crust is golden. Serves 6

Italian Beef

Peggy Nelson from "Whites of San Marco," shares this favorite with us.

5 lbs. beef (a cut of roast)
2-3 Tbsp. Italian Seasoning
2 bay leaves
2 cups water
½ - 1 tsp. garlic powder

Preheat oven to 350°. Mix all ingredients together and pour over meat. Bake 3-4 hours. Baste meat several times during baking.

 Sauce for dipping meat and hard rolls.

1 pkg. au jus
1 can beef consumme or juice from meat

SWEET CHOPS

4 pork chops
(½" to ¾" thick)
1 Tbsp. oil
1 clove garlic,
   minced
1 Tbsp. chopped
   fresh ginger

Sauce:
2 tsp. oil
4 Tbsp. rice wine
4 Tbsp. soy sauce
2 Tbsp. brown sugar

¼ tsp.
   crushed
   red pepper
2 tsp. cornstarch
2 Tbsp. water

Heat oil in skillet. Sauté chops with garlic and ginger in oil,
turning chops to brown both sides. To make sauce, combine oil,
rice wine, soy sauce, brown sugar, and red pepper. Pour
sauce over chops in skillet and cover tightly. Simmer over
low heat until chops are tender and cooked through, 30-35
minutes. Add water as needed to keep sauce from cooking
down too much. Remove chops to serving platter. Stir in cornstarch
dissolved in water. Cook until thickened. Pour over chops and serve.

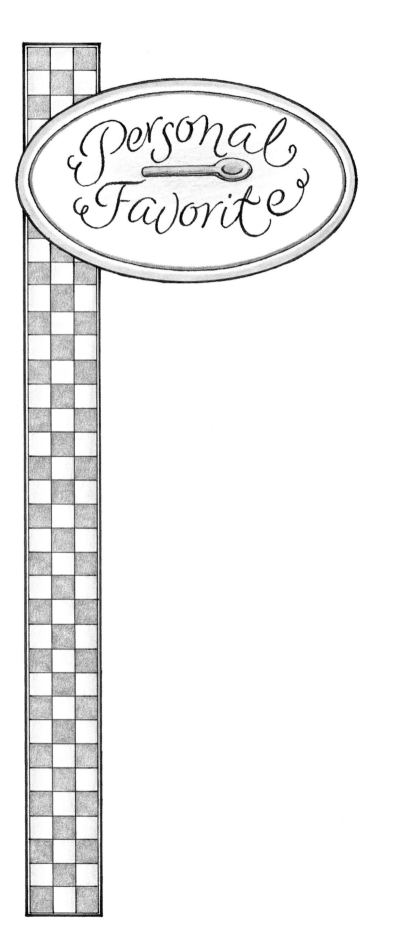

SIDE DISHES

Heart's Desire
Vidalia Onion Casserole

Trudy Yancey, owner of Your Heart's Desire
in Ocala, Florida, somehow managed to find the time
to share this wonderful recipe with us. Her time is
especially precious since it is spread between two stores,
eight children and one (thank goodness) husband.
I wish you could see the photo Trudy sent to us of
her family ~ each of the ten people in this picture
have incredibly beautiful smiles. Perhaps
the reason she is so organized and her
family appears to be so happy is because
she has found her "heart's desire"
in how she is working and
raising her family.

4-5 large Vidalia onions
Parmesan cheese
crispy buttery crackers
margarine as needed

Peel and slice onions. Sauté in small amount
of margarine until limp or opaque. Pour ½ of onions
into casserole dish. Cover with parmesan cheese,
then crushed crackers. Repeat layers and bake
uncovered in 325° oven about 30 minutes.

"Delight yourself in the Lord and
He will give you the desires of your heart." Psalms 37:4

RUTABAGA SOUFFLÉ

Thank you to Louise and Judy from The Country Sampler in Gainesville, Florida!

♥

1 large rutabaga
1 tsp. sugar
1 cup sour cream
2 Tbsp. butter
salt and pepper to taste
1 tsp. baking powder
2 eggs, separated
bread crumbs
healthy dash of nutmeg

Peel rutabaga and cook with sugar. Mash and measure two cups. Combine rutabaga, sour cream, butter, baking powder, salt, pepper and egg yolks. In separate bowl, beat egg whites until stiff. Fold egg whites into rutabaga mixture. Place mixture into 1½ quart casserole. Sprinkle with bread crumbs and nutmeg. Bake at 350° for 30 minutes. Serves 4-6.

Wild Thing

This is a fun wild rice casserole that serves as a wonderful side dish with fish, chicken or beef. Leftover rice, then, makes a great start for an impromptu soup a few days later.

3 cups cooked wild rice
(prepare with can of french onion soup below and water ~ these two liquids together should add up to the amount of liquid listed on the rice package directions.)
8 oz. fresh mushrooms, sliced
1 can french onion soup
⅓ cup chopped celery
¼ cup chopped sweet red pepper
1 clove garlic, minced
¼ cup butter, melted
½ cup slivered almonds
½ cup shredded jack cheese
salt and pepper to taste

In a medium-size skillet, saute the mushrooms, onion, celery, red pepper and garlic in butter until vegetables are tender. In a 2-quart casserole, combine the cooked wild rice, vegetable mixture, almonds, cheese, salt and pepper. Cover and bake in a 325° oven for 35-40 minutes. Serves 6-8.

Down and Dirty RICE

This is another recipe from Kay Routh,
(beloved mom of my friend, Tammy). It is very much like
"Wild Thing", but quite a bit faster to prepare. We thought
you would enjoy having both options when looking for a
"nice-rice" recipe.

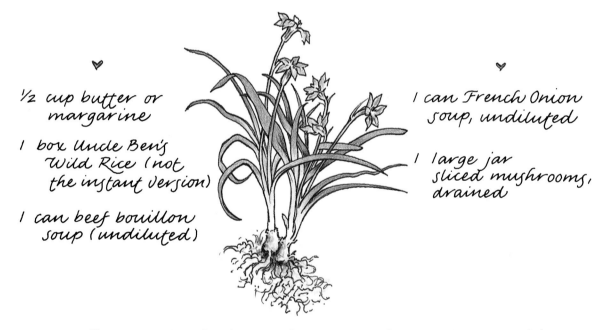

½ cup butter or
   margarine

1 box Uncle Ben's
   Wild Rice (not
   the instant version)

1 can beef bouillon
   soup (undiluted)

1 can French Onion
   soup, undiluted

1 large jar
   sliced mushrooms,
   drained

Brown rice in butter in large skillet. Then combine
with remaining ingredients in a 2-quart casserole dish.
Bake at 325° for 1 hour.

Hint: For a little extra zip, you may throw in the
contents of the seasoning packet that comes with the rice
as you are mixing the rest of the ingredients... or save it
to season your next pot of beef or chicken-based soup.

Sliced Baked Potatoes

Here's an easy and delicious twist to the ordinary baked potato.

4 medium-sized white baking potatoes

1½ tsp. salt and freshly ground pepper to taste

3-4 Tbsp. melted butter

3-4 Tbsp. chopped chives or parsley

2 tsp. dried herbs of your choice (thyme, sage, rosemary, etc.)

4 Tbsp. grated Cheddar cheese

2 Tbsp. grated Parmesan cheese

O.N.E Scrub potatoes well. Cut into thin slices, but not all the way through. You may want to try and lay a wooden spoon directly in front of the potato you are cutting to guard against the knife cutting all the way through.

T.W.O Put potatoes in baking dish. Fan them apart slightly. Sprinkle with salt and pepper, then drizzle with butter. Sprinkle with herbs.

T.H.R.E.E Bake at 425° for about 45-50 minutes. Remove from oven. Sprinkle with cheeses. Bake for another 10-15 minutes or until lightly browned. Check for doneness with a fork.

ZANEY BROCCOLI

I will never forget the day I met Zane (Frances) McCubbin. We were freshmen on the campus of a small mid-western college. It was a beautiful fall day, I thought it was fitting that this spunky, wirey girl, dressed in tastefully faded overalls and a flannel shirt, be named Zane. She has been the energy source for a small group of us who have remained friends over the past 20 years. It did not surprise me that she gave this recipe to me, written on the back of a Jockey underwear package label. After all these years, she still makes me smile. We love you, Zane!

2 (10 oz.) pkgs. frozen chopped broccoli

1 can cream of mushroom soup

1 cup mayonnaise

1 cup grated cheddar cheese

2 eggs, beaten

1 Tbsp. chopped onion

salt and pepper to taste

1 cup crushed butter-
flavored crackers

Cook broccoli and drain. Mix other ingredients (except crackers) and fold into broccoli. Top with crackers. Bake at 400° for 20-30 minutes.

Zane's Dalmations,
Jack and Bob

Madison County POTATOES

Madison County, Iowa is famous for more than just its romantic covered bridges... It's also the home of some great cooks, and happens to be where Shelly's sweet mother, Pat, learned to make these hearty scalloped potatoes. Whip up a batch the next time you feel the need to enjoy one of the "world's great comfort foods".

6 medium-sized potatoes, thinly sliced

1½ tsp. salt

⅛ tsp. pepper

4 Tbsp. flour

3 Tbsp. butter

½ cup cheddar cheese ♥ milk

½ medium-sized onion

1 cup diced ham

onion and garlic powder

Put ⅓ of potato slices in a greased 2 qt. casserole. Sprinkle with ⅓ of onions and ⅓ of blended flour, salt and pepper, and a dash of both garlic and onion powder. Over this add ⅓ diced ham and shredded cheese. Dot with 1 tsp. butter here and there. Repeat layering twice more ending with butter. Pour milk over potatoes until you see it rise. Cover casserole. Bake at 350° for 30-45 minutes or until potatoes are tender. Remove cover. Dot with butter and cheese. Bake until golden, (a few minutes). Remove from oven and let stand 5 minutes before serving.

The WOODENICKEL 5¢
Pasta Dish

Shelly and I
had the pleasure of visiting many of our customers' shops
in the past few years as we were promoting the cookbook,
"Just a Matter of Thyme". The Woodenickel, in Pacific Grove,
California stands out as one of the most "customer friendly"~
not to mention, one of the most beautiful. This particular
recipe is one that owner, Nancy Eadington, favors.

6 - 8 vine-ripe tomatoes
5 cloves garlic
½ cup chopped peppers (red, green or yellow)
1 cup chopped red onion
¼ cup chopped parsley
¼ cup chopped fresh basil
4 - 5 Tbsp. olive oil
3/4 lb. pasta ~ any kind you like

Boil tomatoes for 1 minute in large pot long enough
to loosen the skins. Drain and peel off skins. In a large
skillet sauté onion, peppers, garlic, parsley, basil in
oil until slightly "brown". Cut tomatoes in chunks and
add to skillet. Heat through. Cook pasta according to
directions on package. Drain. Add vegetables and toss lightly.

Note from Nancy: Being a vegetarian and learning to
eat "live" foods has been a goal of mine for many years.
Although most men I know want the traditional
thick sauce... I've never met a lady that would turn
this dish down. (p.s. I'm not much of a cook, but
this dish never fails!)

JoAnn's Spinach

A very special thanks to Joann Ebert, (mother of Anne and Julie from our office) for this scrumptious side dish recipe!

4 (10 oz.) pkgs. frozen spinach
    (thawed and drained)
2 (8 oz.) pkgs. cream cheese
¾ cup margarine
2 (8 oz.) cans artichoke hearts
    (drained and quartered)
½ cup Parmesan cheese
18-24 crushed buttery crackers

Melt together cream cheese and margarine (mixture will be lumpy). Put spinach in a 9 × 13" casserole and spread cream cheese mixture over top. Then, evenly distribute artichoke hearts, cheese and crackers over this mixture. Cover and bake 20 minutes at 350°. Serves 8~10.

Suzan's SPINACH ROCKEFELLAR

The following recipe is from Suzan ("Scarey") Carey, a valued employee at Among Friends. Suzan isn't scarey at all, but one of the most delightful people you will ever have the pleasure of meeting.

1 can drained stewed tomatoes
1 package chopped spinach, cooked
2 Tbsp. butter
1 chopped onion
1 cup bread crumbs
¼ cup parmesan cheese
2 eggs, beaten
season with garlic salt

Sauté onion in butter. Place one can drained stewed tomatoes in bottom of casserole. Top with mixture of spinach, onion and butter, bread crumbs, cheese and eggs. Season with garlic salt. Bake at 350° until heated through (about 20 minutes).

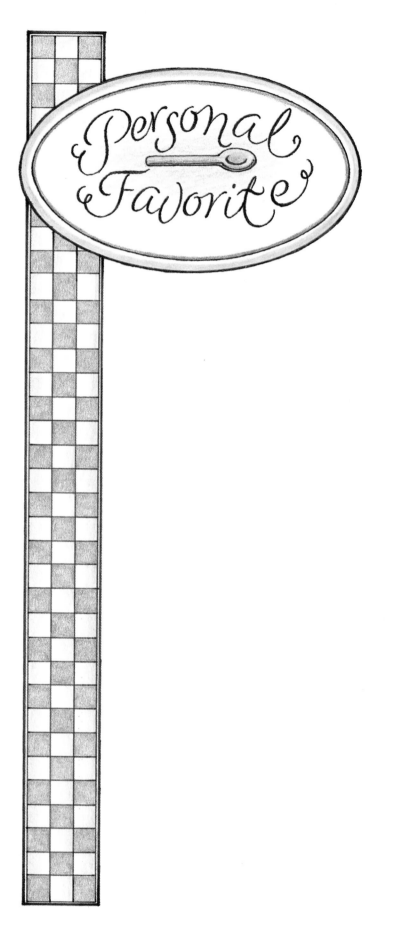

DESSERTS

Summer Breeze

This cookie bar recipe was created by Joyce Schardt, while she was managing a breakfast room we used to have called Wickerleigh's Porch. It was a perfect summertime dessert for our resort area business, where people used to come to enjoy the hand-painted porch floor and the airy wicker furniture, not to mention all of Joyce's refreshing treats. Joyce is now a valued Among Friends employee, lending her creative abilities in a new way. It seems her talents and devotion to our company are endless. You must enjoy this dessert with a tall glass of lemonade or iced tea while sitting out on your porch... that's how Joyce would serve it!

2 cups flour
½ cup sifted confectioners sugar
1 cup butter
4 beaten eggs
2 cups granulated sugar

⅓ cup lemon juice
¼ cup flour
½ tsp. baking powder
1 pint blueberries
1 recipe Cream Cheese filling (next page)

Sift together flour and confectioners sugar. Cut in butter until mixture clings together. Press in two 7" x 11" baking pans. Bake at 350° for 20-25 minutes until lightly browned. Beat eggs until frothy. Add granulated sugar and lemon juice. Sift together ¼ cup flour and baking powder and stir into egg mixture. Spread a layer of cream cheese filling over baked and cooled crust. Sprinkle blueberries over this layer and cover with egg mixture. Bake for 25 minutes.

♡ Cut into squares and sprinkle with confectioner's sugar just prior to serving.

CREAM CHEESE FILLING

This is one of   the most versatile little recipes you will ever use. It can be folded into a brownie batter, tucked inside a loaf of nutbread, drizzled over a coffeecake ~ the possibilities are almost endless. You will find reference to it several times throughout this book... enjoy!

8 oz. cream cheese, softened
6 Tbsp. sugar
1 egg
½ tsp. vanilla

Mix cream cheese until smooth and creamy. Add egg and vanilla and beat well. Store any extra filling in the refrigerator until ready to use. Keeps several weeks.

85

Raz-ma-taz
BROWNIE WEDGES

This is a fun brownie dessert that makes you look like you really know what you're doing in the kitchen. It should be served in the most grand style — presentation is everything here. Just a simple white plate provides the background for this work of art.

Brownie Recipe

4 oz. unsweetened chocolate
½ cup lightly salted butter, room temperature
1⅓ cup sugar
½ tsp. vanilla
3 large eggs, room temperature
3/4 cup flour
½ cup chopped pecans, optional

Lightly grease a 9" round cake pan and preheat oven to 325°. Melt the chocolate and butter in the micro-wave on medium heat, stirring every 30 seconds as not to scorch. Cool.

Blend sugar and chocolate mixture for about 30 seconds. Add vanilla and eggs (one at a time), and blend well. Add flour and mix for another 30 seconds. Stir in nuts. Spread the batter evenly in the greased pan. Bake 30-35 minutes. Cool for at least 1 hour.

Raspberry Fudge Sauce

¼ cup sweetened condensed milk
2 Tbsp. seedless raspberry "spreadable fruit"
(found in the jam and jelly section of your grocery)
1 oz. unsweetened chocolate
3 Tbsp. milk
fresh or individually frozen raspberries for garnish

Melt chocolate with sweetened condensed milk in the microwave GENTLY, stirring every 30 seconds. Use medium setting for this step. Add spreadable fruit and milk and stir until creamy. You may want to heat an additional 15-20 seconds in the microwave. If the mixture is too thick to "drizzle", add a little milk. If it is too thin, add a little more "spreadable fruit".

To Assemble & Serve

Cut brownies into wedges, (thick enough to stand up on a plate but not too thick ~ since this is very rich). Place on dessert plate. Drizzle with chocolate mixture back and forth across from side to side. Line up 3 raspberries down the length of the wedge on top of the chocolate sauce. Make a pool of fudge sauce off to the side of the wedge on the plate and drop 3 raspberries in the center of the pool. M-m-m-m. Enjoy!

Grandma Milligan's Iced Oatmeal Cookies

This is a wonderful family recipe from Anne and Julie's grandmother... sure to become a favorite of yours!

1 cup butter or margarine
2 cups sugar
2 eggs
1½ Tbsp. honey
2 tsp. vanilla

2 cups flour
1½ tsp. baking soda
2 tsp. cinnamon
½ tsp. salt
2 cups quick oats

Cream together butter and sugar; add eggs, honey and vanilla. Combine flour, baking soda, cinnamon, and salt. Gradually add to creamed mixture. Stir in oats. Drop by teaspoonfuls onto ungreased cookie sheets. Bake at 350° for 6-7 minutes. Cool for about a minute on wire rack. Then ice with a thick powdered sugar glaze.

Glaze: Mix about 1 cup powdered sugar and 2 Tbsp. milk until smooth.

Helpful hint: Ice cookies on waxed paper for easy clean up!

The chip chop cookie

To make this unique version of the timeless chocolate chip cookie, you need to select your favorite combination of "chips" (I used semi-sweet and white chocolate chips), then "chop" the oats in your blender or food-processor until it becomes flour. If you have no blender, you may substitute oat flour from the grocery shelf in its place in the recipe. Either way, these are great with a tall glass of cold milk!

♥

1 cup butter, room temperature
1 cup sugar
1 cup brown sugar
2 eggs
1 tsp. vanilla
2 cups all-purpose flour
2½ cups oats, measured and then "powdered" in a blender

½ tsp. salt
1 tsp. baking powder
1 tsp. baking soda
12 oz. semi-sweet chocolate chips
12 oz. white chocolate chips
1 cup chopped nuts

Cream butter and sugars. Add eggs and vanilla. Mix the flour, oats, salt, baking powder and baking soda. Add to the creamed mixture; mixing well. Stir in chips and nuts. Scoop "golf ball size" portions of dough onto ungreased cookie sheets about 2 inches apart.

Bake at 375° for about 8-10 minutes. Makes about 60 cookies.

CARAMEL LAYER
Chocolate Squares

We find at Among Friends that we are often "on the same wave length", so to speak. Perhaps you have experienced this phenomenon with a close friend or family member, where you are so in tune with each other's thoughts that you sometimes wonder if verbal communication is even neccessary... Several times it has happened that I have gone looking for someone in their office, only to discover they are not there, but waiting for me in my office. While we are on the subject, it seems our tastes in food are "in sync" as well, since this yummy bar cookie recipe was submitted by both Candy and Suzan.

1 (14 oz.)pkg. caramels
1 pkg. German Chocolate cake mix
3/4 cup butter, melted
2/3 cup evaporated milk, divided in equal portions
1 cup chocolate chips

Combine caramels and half of evaporated milk. Cook over low heat, stirring often until melted and smooth. Grease 9 x 13" pan. Combine dry cake mix, butter and rest of the evaporated milk, and chocolate chips. Stir just until mixed. Press half of dough firmly in pan. Bake 6 minutes at 350°. Spread caramel mixture over all. Top with remaining half of dough. Spread gently to cover. Bake at 350° for 15 minutes. Let stand until cool before cutting.

Emily's Fudgey Wudgey Cookies

Our neighbor, Emily Wall, named these chocolate cookies for us. They're wonderful with a scoop of vanilla ice cream!

1½ cups firmly packed brown sugar
1 cup softened butter
1 egg
3/4 cup chocolate chips, melted and cooled
2 tsp. vanilla

4 cups all-purpose flour
1 tsp. salt
1 cup chopped nuts, optional
1½ cups sifted powdered sugar

Heat oven to 350°. In a small bowl, combine flour and salt. Set aside. In a large mixer bowl, combine brown sugar and butter. Beat at medium speed, scraping bowl often, until light and fluffy (1-2 min.). Add egg and beat well. Add melted chocolate and vanilla, then flour mixture and continue beating, scraping bowl often until well-mixed. Stir in nuts, if desired. Shape rounded teaspoons of dough into 1-inch balls. Place ½-inch apart on ungreased cookie sheets. Bake for 8-10 minutes or until set. Cool 5 minutes on cookie sheet. Carefully remove. Cool another 5 minutes. Roll in powdered sugar while still warm and again when cool. Makes about 8 dozen.

Cut-Out Cookies

For more than 20 years,
every third grader to pass through
Ann Sasser's class was privileged enough
to enjoy these old-fashioned treats. Ann's collection
of cookie cutters are a special part of this family tradition.
Each one of her children and grandchildren have their
personal favorite that not only creates a cookie, but
cuts out a sweet memory of carefree childhood days
as well. Thank You to Jori, Jimona and
Tami, (Ann's daughters) for sharing
this recipe with us.

Sift together:
2 ¼ cups flour
2 ¼ tsp. baking powder
1 tsp. cinnamon
3/4 tsp. salt
½ tsp. cloves
½ tsp. nutmeg

Cream together:
Cream well
½ cup butter or margarine
3/4 cup sugar

Blend in 1 egg and
¼ cup molasses

Stir in dry ingredients;
mix thoroughly. Chill dough for easier handling.
Roll out on floured surface ⅓ at a time to
1/16 inch thickness. Cut with floured cutters or
pastry wheel into various shapes. Place on
greased baking sheets. Bake 5-7 minutes
in a 400° oven.

CLINTON COOKIES

My sister, Jan, shared this recipe with me recently. Although we can't be sure, we suspect these cookies might be a favorite of a guy named Bill who lives in a big white house.

 Mix together in a medium-size bowl:
    1½ cups all-purpose flour
    1 tsp. salt
    1 tsp. baking soda
    2 cups old-fashioned oats

 In a separate bowl cream together:
    1 cup vegetable oil margarine
    ½ cup sugar
    1 cup light brown sugar

 Add and mix well:
    2 eggs
    1 tsp. vanilla

 Blend in the flour mixture from above and stir in:
    12 oz. chocolate chips

 Drop by teaspoonful onto an ungreased cookie sheet about 2 inches apart, and bake at 350 degrees until golden brown. Makes about 6 dozen.

White Chocolate Raspberry Cake

This cake was the fantasy of one of our wedding customers at "On the Rise". We topped it off with White Chocolate Cream Cheese Frosting (see next page), and garnished it with fresh white roses and a touch of asparagus fern. You don't need wedding bells in your future to include this dessert in your plans.

1¾ cups all-purpose flour
2 tsp. baking powder
¼ tsp. salt
3 oz. white chocolate bar, chopped
¾ cup milk

⅓ cup butter or margarine
1 cup sugar
1 tsp. vanilla
4 eggs
2 cups fresh or frozen raspberries

⅓ cup seedless raspberry jam

Combine flour, baking powder, and salt in a small mixing bowl and set aside. Melt white chocolate with about half of the milk in a small, heavy saucepan over very low heat, stirring constantly until chocolate starts to melt. Remove from heat and stir until it is completely melted and smooth. Stir in remaining milk. Cool.

In a large mixing bowl, beat the butter with an electric mixer until soft and smooth. Add sugar and vanilla; beat well. Add eggs, one at a time, beating until well-combined. Alternately add the flour mixture and the white chocolate mixture, beating on low speed after each addition just until combined.

Spread batter into 2 greased and lightly floured 8 x 1½-inch round baking pans. Bake in 350° oven for 25-30 minutes. Cool in pans on wire racks for 10 minutes before removing from pans.

(♥ See next page for frosting recipe and directions on assembling. Makes about 10 servings. ♥)

White Chocolate Frosting

4 oz. white baking bar, chopped
4 oz. white baking bar, shaved into curls for garnish
8 oz. cream cheese, softened
½ cup butter, room temperature
up to 2 pounds powdered sugar
1 tsp. vanilla

Melt broken pieces of white chocolate in the microwave on a medium setting stirring every 30 seconds, (or in the top of a double boiler). Cool slightly and combine with cream cheese and butter and vanilla. Mix until smooth. Gradually add powdered sugar and continue beating until smooth and stiff. To frost cake, spread bottom layer with jam, then with frosting. Add second layer and repeat. Cover sides evenly with frosting, and garnish with chocolate curls and fresh raspberries. (To make curls, warm chocolate bar in your hand, then run a vegetable peeler down the length of the bar. Keep curls on a piece of waxed paper in a cool place until ready to use.)

German Chocolate
COFFEE·CAKE

Mix well with
an electric mixer:

♥

1 box Swiss or
German Chocolate
Cake Mix

2 eggs, beaten

1 stick butter or margarine,
melted

½ cup chopped pecans

½ cup shredded
coconut

Spread above
mixture into a
greased 9 x 13" pan.

Combine the following and spread over the
top of the chocolate mixture:

2 eggs, beaten

8 oz. cream cheese, softened

1 tsp. vanilla

1 pound powdered sugar (about 4 cups)

Bake at 350° for 30-35 minutes. Cool. Sprinkle
with powdered sugar before serving.

Serves about 20. Very rich!

♥

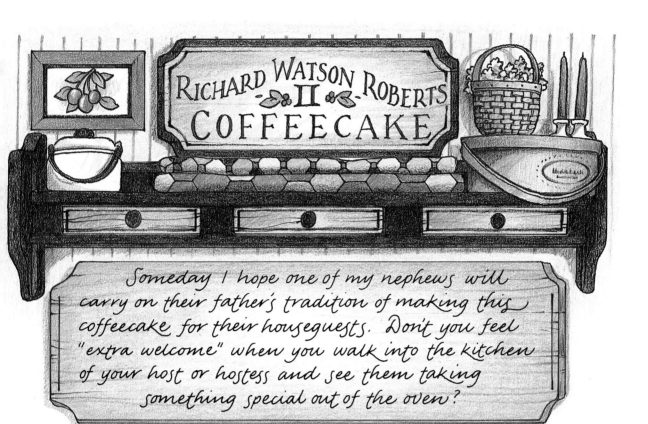

RICHARD WATSON ROBERTS II COFFEECAKE

Someday I hope one of my nephews will carry on their father's tradition of making this coffeecake for their houseguests. Don't you feel "extra welcome" when you walk into the kitchen of your host or hostess and see them taking something special out of the oven?

½ cup butter, softened
8 oz. cream cheese, softened
1¼ cups sugar
2 eggs
1 tsp. vanilla

2 cups flour
1 tsp. baking powder
½ tsp. baking soda
¼ tsp. salt
⅓ cup milk

Topping:

½ cup brown sugar
½ cup flour

3 Tbsp. butter
1 tsp. cinnamon

Cream butter, cream cheese and sugar until light. Add eggs and vanilla. Beat well. Stir together dry ingredients in a separate bowl. Add to creamed mixture alternately with milk, beating until smooth after each addition. Spread in greased 9" x 13" pan. Combine topping ingredients and sprinkle over cake. Bake in a 350° oven for about 30-35 minutes, or until light golden brown.

Peaches & Cream
BRUNCH CAKE

This cake recipe is designed to help you exercise your creativity. You may use peaches, as described below, or select one of many fresh or frozen fruits to replace the peaches. Sometimes when I really feel like "pushing the envelope", I'll even mix two fruits into the batter. Some ideas to get your creative juices flowing: peeled and chopped apples*, blueberries, diced apricots, raspberries, etc...

2 cups flour
1 tsp. baking soda
1 tsp. salt
1 cup packed brown sugar
2/3 cup chopped nuts
1 tsp. cinnamon
1/2 tsp. nutmeg

1/2 cup butter, softened
1 cup sugar
1 tsp. vanilla
3 eggs
8 oz. sour cream
2 cups peeled and chopped peaches

1 recipe Cream Cheese filling (p. 85)

 Stir together flour, baking soda, and salt ; set aside. In a second bowl, mix brown sugar, nuts, cinnamon, and nutmeg; set aside.

 In a large mixing bowl, beat butter and sugar together until well-blended. Add vanilla and beat until fluffy. Add eggs, one at a time, beating well after each. Beat in sour cream. Add flour mixture and beat until smooth. Fold in peaches by hand.

 Spread half of the batter in a greased 13 x 9 x 2" baking pan. Sprinkle half of the brown sugar mixture evenly over batter. Drop cream cheese filling by the teaspoonful evenly over this. Drop remaining batter by the spoonful on top. Sprinkle with remaining brown sugar mixture. Bake in a 350° oven for about 30-35 minutes or until tester comes out clean.
Serves 12-15.

* Try the apple version of this in the fall, and add a light drizzle of caramel ice cream topping over the surface of the cake right before serving.

BLUEBERRY-ORANGE Coffee cake

This is a wonderful addition for a special weekend breakfast or brunch because it is so quick and easy to make.

13 oz. box Blueberry Muffin mix, prepared according to the directions (this usually requires an egg and some water).

11 oz. can Mandarin oranges, drained

1/4 cup flour

1/4 cup sugar

1 tsp. cinnamon

2 Tbsp. butter or margarine

1/2 cup chopped pecans (optional)

Before preparing the muffin mix, take a moment to make the topping for the coffee cake. Mix flour, sugar, and cinnamon together in a small bowl. Cut in butter until mixture is crumbly. Add pecans and stir gently. Set aside.

Prepare the muffin mix according to the package. Fold in well-drained blueberries and oranges until just blended. Turn into a greased 8"-square or round cake pan. Sprinkle cinnamon topping over all and bake in a 400° oven for 20-25 minutes. Serve warm with a pat of butter on top. Makes 6-8 servings.

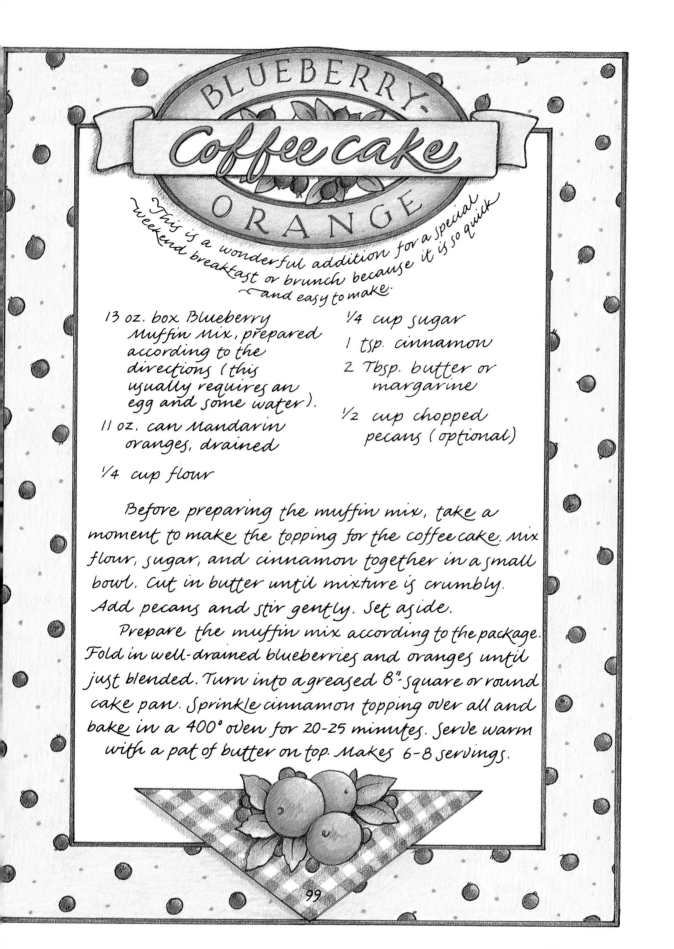

Caramel Pecan Torte

This recipe comes to us from our sales representatives in Seattle, Washington. Jim and Karen Corcoran (of Northbay Marketing fame) are not only gifted in the area of sales, but also in the kitchen! The next two recipes are desserts that Karen serves often...

1½ cups flour
¼ tsp. salt
⅓ cup sugar

6 Tbsp. cold butter, cut into pieces
3 egg yolks, lightly beaten (save whites)
½ tsp. vanilla

1. Mix together flour, salt, and sugar. Cut in the butter until mixture resembles corn meal and there are no butter chunks.

2. Combine egg yolks, vanilla, and 2 Tbsp. water and mix with the flour until it just begins to hold together when you press it in your hand. Add more water, only as needed.

3. Press and form the dough into a flat round. Wrap and chill at least one hour.

Filling:

1 cup sugar

¼ cup light corn syrup

4 Tbsp. butter

⅔ cup heavy cream

2 cups chopped pecans

2 tsp. honey

1½ tsp. Chambord liqueur

1. Combine sugar, 2½ Tbsp. water and corn syrup in heavy saucepan. Cook over low heat a few minutes, stirring occasionally, until sugar has dissolved.

2. Cover pan, raise heat to medium and cook 10-15 minutes until mixture is caramelized or has turned an amber color. Do not stir while it is cooking, but swirl the pan occasionally.

3. Add 4 Tbsp. butter and stir until dissolved, then add cream and pecans. Boil gently for about 5 minutes or until thickened slightly. Cool for about 10 minutes. Stir in honey and Chambord. Cool to room temperature.

To Assemble:

1. Preheat oven to 350°. Grease and flour an 8" by 1½" cake pan.

2. Working on a floured surface, divide the dough into two portions, one slightly larger than the other. Roll the larger piece in a round that will fit into the bottom and sides of the pan. Press this round gently into the pan and brush all surfaces with the reserved egg white.

3. Pour cooled filling into the pan. Roll out the other portion of dough to fit the top. Brush the top edge of the bottom crust with more egg white. Lay the second round of dough on top and press the edges together to form a seal.

4. Bake 30 minutes or until surface is lightly browned. Cool completely. Run a sharp knife around the sides of the torte and de-pan into a serving platter.

5. When ready to serve, prepare the glaze below and spread on top and sides of torte. Garnish with pecan halves and chill about 10-20 minutes to set the glaze.

Glaze:

Melt 6 oz. chocolate chips and 4 Tbsp. butter in the microwave GENTLY (or in top of double boiler). Stir until smooth and cool slightly.

Austrian Sachertorte

from Lisa's Tea Treasures℠

Type and size of cooking container: Butter and flour two 8" x 1½" cake pans.

Temperature: Preheat the oven to 350°.

Number of Servings: 12

Preparation Time: 30 - 45 minutes

Cooking Time: Bake for 40 to 50 minutes, or until a toothpick inserted in the center comes out clean.

Cake Ingredients:

- 4 Tbsp. brewed Tea Lisa's Tea Treasures The Baron's Choice (Chocolate Apricot Tea Blend)
- 8 oz. dark sweet chocolate (either semisweet or bittersweet is acceptable)
- 8 Tbsp. butter
- 8 egg yolks
- 1 tsp. vanilla extract
- 8 egg whites
- 3/4 cup granulated sugar
- 1 cup all-purpose flour
- 3/4 cup apricot jam

Icing Ingredients:

- 8 oz. dark sweet chocolate (semi-sweet)
- 3/4 cup whipping cream
- 2 tsp. of Brewed Lisa's Tea Treasures The Baron's Choice Tea Blend
- 2 Tbsp. light corn syrup

Procedure:

To make the cake, melt the chocolate and butter in the top of a double boiler and remove from the heat. Allow the chocolate to cool slightly. Stir in the egg yolks, beat slightly, and add the vanilla and brewed tea. Set aside to cool.

Beat the egg whites until frothy. Add the sugar slowly, a tablespoon at a time, still whipping, until the whites are stiff enough to hold firm peaks; they should hold their shape.

Mix one-third of the beaten egg whites into the chocolate mixture to soften it, then pour the chocolate back over the egg whites. Sprinkle the flour over all and fold it in gently.

When the chocolate is well-mixed, divide the batter evenly between the two pans. Tap the pans gently to level the batter. When done, cool for 30-45 minutes, then turn the cakes out of the pans onto racks.

To make the icing, melt the chocolate, whipping cream, brewed tea and corn syrup in a small saucepan or the top of a double boiler. Remove from the heat and cool slightly.

Heat the apricot jam and, using a long spatula, spread the jam over the top of the cake. Invert the second layer over the first. Pour chocolate icing over the cake. It should be runny enough to spread smoothly.

If desired, whipping cream can be used to decorate the cake. Whip the cream with powdered sugar and vanilla. Dollop in mounds on the top of the cake or use a pastry bag to decorate. The cream was traditionally used to cut the intensity of the chocolate.

A special thanks to Lisa Strauss, the president and founder of Lisa's Tea Treasures in San Jose, CA., for sharing the secret of one of their most treasured recipes. Passed down to Lisa from her Austrian grandmother, this recipe is sure to become a memorable experience for you and your guests. Lisa invites you to call their toll-free number, 1-800-500-4TEA, to order the chocolate apricot tea used in this recipe or to inquire about any of their fourteen locations.

Marble Cheese

T · O · R · T · E

*Grace your table
with this very elegant dessert...
perfect for a bridal shower or
any extra-special occasion.
It is best if made the day before.*

Crust Ingredients:

- 4 Tbsp. butter
- 2 Tbsp. brown sugar
- 3/4 cup flour
- 1/4 cup chopped pecans

Glaze Ingredients:

- 1/4 cup heavy cream
- 1 Tbsp. sugar
- 1 Tbsp. butter
- 3/4 cup chocolate chips
- 3 Tbsp. strong coffee

Filling Ingredients:

- 4 (8 oz.) pkgs. cream cheese, softened
- 1 cup sugar
- 2 Tbsp. flour
- 1 Tbsp. vanilla
- 5 eggs
- 1/2 cup heavy cream

104

Marble Cheese Torte

To Make Crust:

Preheat oven to 350°. Cream butter and brown sugar together. Mix in flour and pecans. Press dough into bottom of a 9" springform pan. Bake 15 minutes, then allow to cool while you make filling.

To Make Filling:

Blend cream cheese with sugar, flour and vanilla until smooth. Add eggs and continue beating until creamy. Mix in heavy cream.

To Make Glaze:

Combine 1/4 cup heavy cream, sugar and butter in a saucepan and heat on low until boiling. Boil one minute. Then wisk in chocolate chips and stir until shiny. Then stir in coffee.

Pour filling into crust. Drizzle 3 Tbsp. of glaze over surface of filling, then swirl the filling with a knife, criss-crossing the glaze throughout. Reserve remaining glaze until later. Bake 50-55 minutes until set. Cool to room temperature and then chill thoroughly. When ready to glaze, press down all over top of cheesecake with fingertips to push cracks together and even out surface. If necessary, reheat glaze to spreading consistency. Pour over the surface and spread evenly. Chill to set. Sprinkle with chopped pecans and serve.

CHRISTMAS COMFORT CAKE

The Annual Christmas Open House at "Shirley's Home" in Exeter, Ca. would not be complete without their signature holiday dessert. ♡

Cake:
18 ½ oz. Duncan Hines Yellow Cake Mix
3 ¾ oz. pkg. Instant Vanilla Pudding
4 eggs
½ cup cold water
½ cup oil
1 cup nuts
½ cup Southern Comfort

Glaze:
¼ cup butter
⅛ cup water
½ cup sugar
¼ cup Southern Comfort

Cake: Combine cake ingredients. Beat at medium speed for 2 minutes. Pour into greased, floured 10 inch tube or 12 cup Bundt pan. Bake at 325° for 1 hour. Cool. Invert on plate. Prick top, brush half of glaze evenly over top and sides. Cool cake. Reheat glaze and brush over cake. Just before serving, sift 1 tablespoon powdered sugar over cake.

Glaze: Melt butter. Stir in water, sugar. Boil 3 minutes, stirring constantly. Remove from heat, stir in Southern Comfort.

Meyer's De MENTHE CAKE

John Meyer, one of our very best sales reps, not only makes "one mean de menthe cake", he is a wonderful host as well. John and Stephanie opened their home to us on countless occasions as we traveled through Oklahoma for various book signings. As we gathered around the family piano and let Shelly serenade us until bedtime, I was reminded of why we love our work so much... and the people it brings into our lives.

Prepare <u>one white cake mix</u>, according to package directions, and add:

<u>3 Tbsp. creme de menthe</u>

Bake as directed.

Let cake cool and top with

<u>one jar</u>
<u>hot fudge sauce</u>

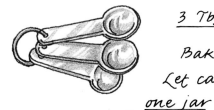

Then mix <u>one large</u>
<u>carton non-dairy</u>
<u>whipped topping</u>

...with <u>3 Tbsp.</u>
<u>creme de menthe</u>
and "frost" cake with it.
Refrigerate until ready to serve.

Note: Just for fun, we garnished with <u>chocolate curls</u> just before serving

Raspberry Fudge Ice Cream Pie

♥ One recipe for graham ~
cracker pie crust (next page)
♥ ½ gallon softened vanilla ice cream
♥ 3 cups fresh or frozen raspberries
♥ 2 small chocolate almond candy bars,
broken into bite-sized pieces
♥ 1 jar hot fudge ice cream topping

After pressing graham cracker crust into pie plate, spoon half of the ice cream over crust. Cover with plastic wrap and very gently smooth ice cream out over bottom of crust evenly. The plastic wrap keeps your hands clean and prevents the crust from breaking up under the ice cream. Add a layer of candy bar pieces, and half of the raspberries. Keep remaining raspberries in the refrigerator until serving time.

Add rest of ice cream and smooth out as before with plastic wrap on top. Keeping plastic wrap over pie, place in the freezer until firm (about 1-2 hours). Cut into wedges. Garnish each piece with remaining raspberries and hot fudge sauce. Makes about 8 servings.

Basic Graham Cracker Crust

Mix together:

1½ cups graham cracker crumbs

6 Tbsp. butter or margarine, melted

¼ cup sugar

Press into bottom and sides of 9" pie plate.

♥ Note: You can get creative with this basic recipe by using chocolate or honey-cinnamon graham crackers (or even a combination of the three!). Just a pinch of nutmeg or cinnamon also adds a nice touch.

The Painted Door Gallery
CHOCOLATE CAKE

If someone were to ask me to reach back in my memory to recall the most action-packed day I've ever spent, one that would come to mind first would be the day that Shelly and I spent at The Painted Door in Oklahoma City. We were invited to Avis' beautiful store to share sample recipes from Just a Matter of Thyme, and to autograph books for her customers. To say that Avis understands the meaning of "customer service" is an understatement. This woman lives it. After hours of smiling, signing, baking, smiling, signing, baking... all of the employees were graced with a pair of "foo-foo" slippers to wear as we finished up. What a picture that made... and what a lesson in sharing yourself through your business.

In a bowl combine:

    2 cups sifted flour
    2 cups sugar
    ½ tsp. salt
    1 tsp. soda

In a saucepan, combine:

    ¼ cup shortening
    1 cup water
    ½ cup butter
    4 Tbsp. cocoa

Heat to boiling and then combine with the above dry ingredients.

Add:

    ½ cup buttermilk
    2 eggs
    1 Tbsp. vanilla

Beat well and pour into greased and floured 9 × 13 × 2" pan. Bake at 425° for 25 minutes (middle of cake will split as it bakes :)

Avis' cake is presented here as a layer cake~ but it's actually much easier than that. So instead of spending a lot of time frosting a cake, you can relax and put on your "foo-foo" slippers ~ just pour the silky glaze over a 9 × 13" version.

Icing: 4 Tbsp. cocoa   ½ cup butter
        4 Tbsp. milk   dash of salt
        1 tsp. vanilla   2/3 box of
                                powdered
                                sugar

Bring cocoa and butter to a boil. Add milk, salt, vanilla and powdered sugar. Mix well until smooth and have ready when cake comes out. Ice while hot. Enjoy!

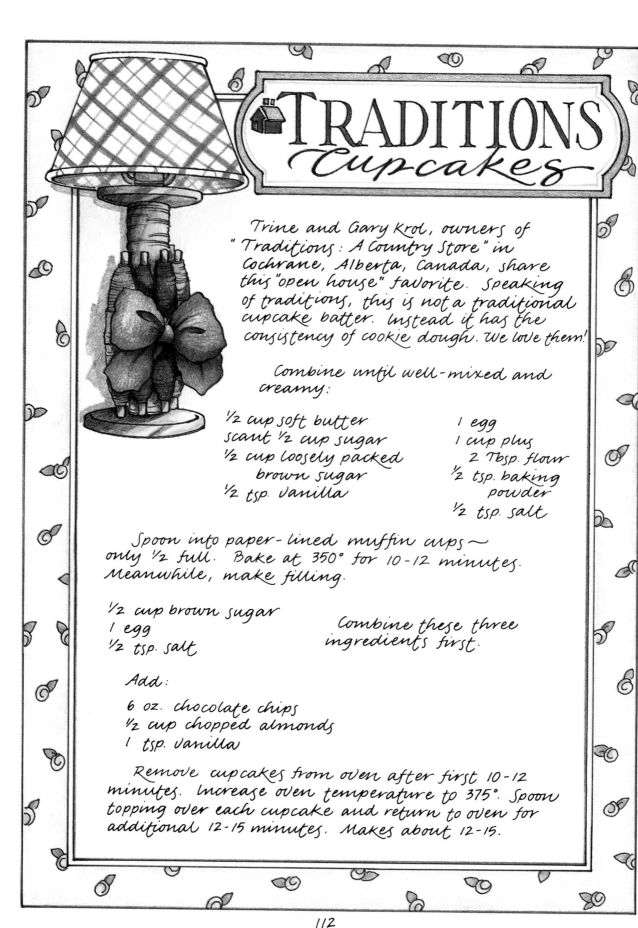

TRADITIONS
cupcakes

Trine and Gary Krol, owners of "Traditions: A Country Store" in Cochrane, Alberta, Canada, share this "open house" favorite. Speaking of traditions, this is not a traditional cupcake batter. Instead it has the consistency of cookie dough. We love them!

Combine until well-mixed and creamy:

½ cup soft butter
scant ½ cup sugar
½ cup loosely packed
    brown sugar
½ tsp. vanilla

1 egg
1 cup plus
    2 Tbsp. flour
½ tsp. baking
    powder
½ tsp. salt

Spoon into paper-lined muffin cups ~ only ½ full. Bake at 350° for 10-12 minutes. Meanwhile, make filling.

½ cup brown sugar
1 egg
½ tsp. salt

Combine these three ingredients first.

Add:

6 oz. chocolate chips
½ cup chopped almonds
1 tsp. vanilla

Remove cupcakes from oven after first 10-12 minutes. Increase oven temperature to 375°. Spoon topping over each cupcake and return to oven for additional 12-15 minutes. Makes about 12-15.

The Apple Core Dumplings

Falba Core and Lynne Core Angle invite you to visit them at The Apple Core gift shop in Jefferson City, (Missouri's stately capitol city), and hope these tasty dumplings will soon become the "apple of your eye".

Crust:

- 2 cups flour
- 1 tsp. salt
- 2 tsp. baking powder
- 3/4 cup crisco
- 1/2 cup milk

Mix in same method as pie crust. Roll 1/4" thick and cut in 5" squares.

Peel and Core:

- 6 Jonathon apples

Place in square of crust. Generously sprinkle with: 1/2 cup sugar, 1/4 tsp. nutmeg, 1 tsp. cinnamon, 1/4 cup butter divided among the 6 apples.

Dampen and fold corners to center pinching edges together. Place in 9" x 13" pan, greased.

Syrup:

Bring to a boil and cook for 3 minutes:

- 1 cup granulated sugar
- 1/2 cup light brown sugar
- 1/2 cup butter
- 1 tsp. cinnamon
- 2 cups water

Pour over dumplings. Bake 35-40 minutes at 375°.

Out of This World PIE

Sometimes it's a good idea to step out of this world and escape to some quiet place — that's what Josephine's customers do in Godfrey, Illinois. Josephine's Tea Room serves this pie with pride.

3/4 cup sugar

1 Tbsp. cornstarch

1 (20 oz.) can pineapple tidbits, undrained

1 (21 oz.) can cherry pie filling

1 tsp. red food coloring (optional)

1 (3 oz.) box strawberry gelatin

4 bananas, peeled and sliced

1 (10-inch) deep pie shell, baked and cooled

3 cups whipped cream or non-dairy whipped topping

1 cup finely chopped pecans

Measure sugar, cornstarch and pineapple into saucepan and mix well. Stir in pie filling and food color. Stir gently to avoid mashing cherries. Cook over medium heat until mixture comes to a boil and is well-thickened, about 5-8 minutes. Remove from heat; stir in dry gelatin. Let cool. Gently stir in bananas. Spoon into pie shell. Cover with whipped cream and garnish with pecans. Refrigerate until pie is set.

Pleasant Company CAKE

This is a coffeecake that is ideal for weekend company. Just put it in the oven Saturday morning, and enjoy the smell of cinnamon floating through the house as everyone rises. I have to say it is hard to imagine Karen Perry, who shares this recipe with us, ever indulging in it. Karen is known for her "dietary discipline" around our office. It's handy for us that her self-discipline shines through in every part of her work as well ~ which makes for very pleasant company. Thank You, Karen!

♥

1 box yellow cake mix
1 (3½ oz.) pkg. vanilla instant pudding
¾ cup oil
¾ cup water
4 eggs
1 tsp. butter extract
1 tsp. vanilla

Layer Filling:

½ cup chopped pecans
¼ cup sugar
2 tsp. cinnamon

Combine cake and pudding mix with oil and water, mixing well at low speed. Add eggs, one at a time, beating well after each. Beat for 6-8 minutes at high speed, adding butter extract and vanilla during last minute.

Mix together filling ingredients in a small bowl. Grease bundt pan and sprinkle a little cinnamon mixture to dust the pan. Pour layer of batter, the rest of the filling, and then the rest of the batter in the pan. Bake at 350° for 40-45 minutes. Cool 8 minutes right side up, then turn over onto a serving plate.

115

CROWD PLEASER

This is a recipe from Suzan's "sweet-sis" in Atlanta ~ she says it has pleased many a crowd...

YEAH! M, M, GOOD... ..GOOD JOB!
THANKS! ...LOVE YA, BABE!

1. Crush 25 oreos.

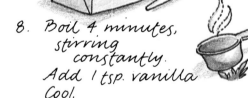

2. Add ¼ cup melted butter

3. Press into 9 x 13" pan.

4. Slice ½ gallon of vanilla ice cream and lay on top of crust.

5. Cover with chopped pecans.

6. Put in freezer.

7. Combine in a saucepan:

4 oz. German sweet chocolate
2/3 cup evaporated milk
½ tsp. salt
2/3 cup sugar
½ cup butter

8. Boil 4 minutes, stirring constantly. Add 1 tsp. vanilla. Cool.

9. Pour sauce over mixture in 9" x 13" pan.

10. Cover with non-dairy whipped topping. Freeze and enjoy!

Ode to an Egg

It seems to me that eggs have really taken a lot of abuse in the past few years. I understand the importance of balance in our dietary lives, and therefore would never suggest that eggs, eaten in excess, would not present a problem for us. However, consider their contribution...

♥ Eggs are not only a tasty food source in the most simple of forms, but they also treat our bodies to protein, riboflavin, iron, vitamins A and D, choline and phosphorus.

♥ The multi-talented egg also serves us in cooking as a leavener in cakes, cookies, breads and souffles, as a base for dressings, a thickener in sauces and custards, and as a coating for breaded or battered foods.

♥ As you celebrate the egg, make sure you use the freshest possible to get the full value ~ a simple test:

Place the suspect egg in at least several inches of water in a bowl. If the egg sinks and lies on its side, it's fresh. If it sinks but stands partially or fully erect and on its tapered end, it is "just over the edge" (technically still edible). If it floats, get rid of it! To ensure the longest life for fresh eggs, store in the refrigerator in its original carton with the wide end up.

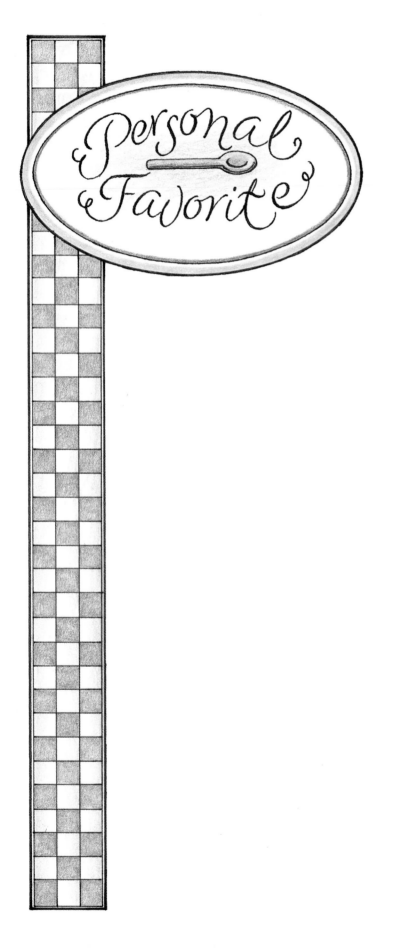

HEART ♥ SMART

♫ ♡ ♫

♫ A book like "Heart and Soul" would not be complete without a chapter devoted to our hearts and good health. When we began our research for this "Heart Smart" collection, we discovered a wealth of good ideas and delicious recipes from our friend and fellow writer, Heather Berry.

The next ten recipes have been graciously contributed by Heather and her husband (and official "tester"), Rick. They are followed by a further collection of truly tasteful dishes that are both easy-to-make and easy-to-love.

Enjoy these with the ones you care about...
Here's to your heart and soul! ♫

This spicy bread is tasty with any peppery dish...

... but if you like your cornbread with a bit less kick, just remove the chili peppers and chili powder.

1 cup yellow cornmeal

¾ cup all-purpose flour

3 Tbsp. sugar

2 tsp. baking powder

¼ tsp. chili powder

Pinch of cayenne pepper (optional)

2 Tbsp. tub-style margarine

¾ cup skim milk

1 large egg white

2 Tbsp. canned mild green chili peppers, well-drained

3 Tbsp. chopped sweet red bell peppers

SOME LIKE IT HOT Cornbread

Preheat oven to 400°. Spray an 8 x 8" baking pan with vegetable spray. In a medium bowl, mix the cornmeal, flour, sugar, baking powder, chili powder and cayenne pepper.

With a fork, cut in the margarine until the mixture resembles coarse meal. Add the milk, egg white, chili peppers and red pepper. Stir well but don't over mix. Put mix in prepared pan. Bake for 17 minutes or until top is lightly browned and a toothpick in the center comes out clean.

Serves: 9

Santa Fe STEW
Missouri Style

3 cups boneless chicken or turkey breasts, cooked and cubed

1 Tbsp. olive and safflower oil

1 large purple onion, finely chopped

½ tsp. garlic powder

¼ tsp. parsley

1 pkg. taco or chili seasoning

3 cans spicy tomatoes, undrained and cut up

½ cup defatted chicken broth

1 can (15 oz.) pinto beans, rinsed and drained

1 can (7 oz.) whole kernel corn, drained

1 can (7 oz.) diced green chiles

In a large skillet, heat oil. Brown chicken or turkey and add onion, garlic powder and parsley. Brown 2 minutes longer. Add remaining ingredients and blend well. Bring to a boil and reduce heat and simmer 25 minutes. (Cook longer for a thicker stew.)

Serves 6.

Good Toppers

Honey Mustard Dressing:

½ cup fat-free mayonnaise
¼ cup honey
¼ cup prepared yellow mustard
⅓ cup apple cider vinegar
¼ tsp. cayenne pepper
½ cup water
1 tsp. minced garlic

Mix all ingredients together and blend well. Chill and serve.

Heatherbee's Favorite Poppyseed Dressing:

⅓ cup purple onion, chopped very fine

1½ cups sugar or equivalent sugar substitute

1 Tbsp. honey

2 tsp. dry mustard

1 tsp. lite salt (optional)

⅔ cup white vinegar

2 cups liquid Butter Buds

2 Tbsp. poppy seeds

Mix all ingredients in a blender until smooth. Serve chilled.

Artichoke Salad

♥ Dressing:

14 oz. artichoke hearts, drained

3 Tbsp. olive oil
1 Tbsp. red wine vinegar
1 Tbsp. chopped onion
2 Tbsp. Honey Dijon mustard
1 clove garlic, minced
½ cup water
Tarragon, to taste
Cracked black pepper

♥ Fresh Romaine lettuce leaves, washed and excess water shaken off

2 cups sweet red pepper or golden bell pepper strips

14 oz. artichoke hearts, drained

2½ cups fat-free cheddar cheese

Cover serving dish with Romaine lettuce. Arrange 14 oz. of artichokes, red pepper and shredded cheese on lettuce. For dressing, combine artichoke hearts, oil, vinegar, onion, mustard and garlic in food processor or blender; process until smooth. Continue to process, gradually adding water. Season to taste with pepper and tarragon. Chill.

Serve over salad.

123

Quick
PASTA PRIMAVERA
a microwave dish

8 oz. uncooked spaghetti
2 Tbsp. reduced-calorie margarine
1 cup each Julienne sliced carrots and zucchini
1 cup fresh, young asparagus, cleaned and cut into 1" pieces
1 cup sliced fresh mushrooms
¼ cup thinly sliced green onions
½ tsp. dried basil leaves
½ tsp. Italian seasoning
1 clove garlic, minced
Freshly ground black pepper, to taste
¾ cup non fat sour cream
¼ cup grated low-calorie Parmesan cheese,
plus ¼ cup for garnish

Prepare spaghetti as directed on package. Rinse with warm water. Drain and place in a medium bowl. Set aside.

In a 2-quart casserole dish, melt margarine in microwave. Stir in carrots, asparagus, zucchini, mushrooms, green onions, garlic and seasonings. Cover. Microwave on high for 6-8 minutes, stirring once, until vegetables are tender-crisp. Pour over spaghetti. Stir together non fat sour cream and cheese. Toss with pasta and vegetables to coat. Reheat right before serving. Serves 8.

CREAMY MUSTARD & SMOKED TURKEY SALAD

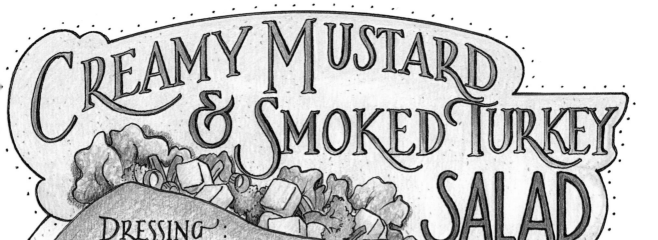

DRESSING:

3 ounces low-fat cream-cheese, softened

¼ cup low-fat dairy sour cream

2 Tbsp. honey

5 tsp. Dijon mustard

1 Tbsp. minced green onion

1 ½ tsp. dried basil

⅛ tsp. each: garlic powder, lite salt and black pepper

SALAD:

3 cups cubed, smoked turkey breast

2 cups raw broccoli flowerets

1 cup julienne red or golden bell peppers

1 - 8 oz. can sliced water chestnuts, drained

Whole wheat pita bread

For dressing, combine all ingredients and mix well. For salad, place all ingredients in a large mixing bowl. Gently toss with dressing. Refrigerate, covered, 1 to 2 hours to allow flavors to blend. Serve in whole wheat pita pockets or over beds of fresh lettuce.

Love Your Heart

There was a brief period of time when I had the privelege to co-own and operate a breakfast room with a very special couple, Jack and Barbara Heiser. We called it Wickerleigh's Porch, and it was anchored by their wonderful store, The Cornerpost. Jack's dream was to offer at least a few really satisfying menu items that met the needs of people who were "cholesterol conscious". "Chef Joyce" came up with this incredibly tasty alternative to Eggs Benedict.

♥

4 whole English Muffins
8 slices low-fat Canadian Bacon
   (yes, it does exist)

12 asparagus spears, cooked
1 fresh tomato, sliced
chives or parsley chopped
   for garnish
paprika

♥

Wickerleigh's Porch
W · E · L · C · O · M · E

Sauce Ingredients:

½ cup low-fat margarine
½ cup flour
⅛ tsp. salt or salt substitute
dash white pepper
15 oz. can chicken broth
¼ cup plain low-fat yogurt
½ tsp. dijon mustard
1 tsp. lemon juice

♥

To make sauce, melt margarine. Blend in flour, salt and pepper. Add broth, wisking constantly until mixture thickens. Stir in mustard, yogurt and lemon juice. Heat through.

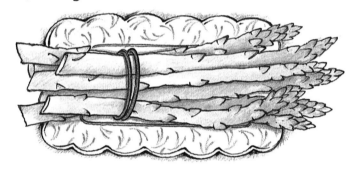

Split English muffins with a fork, toast lightly. Warm Canadian bacon in microwave with cooked asparagus spears. Assemble English muffin with Canadian bacon on top, then tomato slice and asparagus spears. Top with sauce. Garnish with chives or parsley and paprika. Serves 4.

Tip from Joyce: During asparagus season, buy a large quantity to blanch. Place on a cookie sheet to freeze individually. Package in ziplock bags and defrost as needed.

VEGETABLE LASAGNE

This low-fat dish is, hands down, my favorite. It has all the attributes of the fatty versions we are all accustomed to, but leaves you feeling GOOD and satisfied, instead of GUILTY.

1 Tbsp. vegetable oil

3 cups diced eggplant

8 oz. fresh mushrooms, sliced

3/4 cup chopped onions

1 tsp. minced garlic

1 can (28 oz.) crushed tomatoes

1 can (15 oz.) chunky
   tomato sauce

salt to taste

1/2 tsp. sugar

1/2 tsp. basil

1 lb. carrots, peeled and shredded

1 (10 oz.) pkg. frozen spinach,
   thawed and squeezed dry

15 oz. part skim ricotta cheese

1 cup shredded part-skim
   mozzarella cheese

1 large egg, beaten

pinch nutmeg

9 lasagne noodles, cooked
   according to package
   directions

1/4 cup freshly grated
   parmesan cheese

O N E

Heat oil in a large skillet over medium-high heat. Add eggplant, mushrooms, onions and garlic; cook, stirring, 5 minutes.

Stir in tomatoes, tomato sauce, salt, sugar and basil. Bring to a boil; reduce heat to low, cover and simmer until eggplant is tender, (about 20 minutes).

T W O

Meanwhile, preheat oven to 375°. Bring 2 quarts water to a boil in large saucepan. Add carrots and cook one minute. drain. Combine carrots, spinach, ricotta, mozzarella, egg and nutmeg in large bowl.

T H R E E

Spoon 1¼ cup eggplant sauce in 13 x 9 inch baking dish. Layer with 3 lasagne noodles and half the spinach mixture, 3 more noodles and 1¾ cups sauce, then remaining spinach and noodles. Top with remaining sauce. Sprinkle with Parmesan. Bake uncovered 35-40 minutes. Makes 6-8 servings.

Blueberry~Citrus MUFFINS

2 cups sifted all-purpose flour
½ cup sugar
¼ cup brown sugar
1 tsp. baking powder
1 tsp. baking soda
½ tsp. salt
    2 cups fresh blueberries

¼ cup low-calorie margarine
8 oz. plain low-fat (or vanilla) yogurt
1 egg or egg substitute
2 tsp. grated orange rind
½ tsp. lemon extract
2 tsp. vanilla extract

Heat oven to 375°. Line 12 muffin cups with paper baking cups. In a large glass bowl, combine flour, sugars, baking powder, baking soda and salt. Add blueberries and toss to coat with flour and set aside.

In a medium bowl, melt butter in microwave. Cool slightly then add yogurt, egg or egg substitute, orange rind and lemon and vanilla extracts, beat until well-blended.

Stir yogurt mixture into dry mixture until dry ingredients are moistened ~ do not over-stir. Divide batter into muffin cups and bake 20-25 minutes or until muffins spring back to touch. Cool in pan on wire racks 5 minutes.

Remove from muffin cups and serve.

Sinfully Lowfat Peach Cheesecake

- ♥ 1 cup graham cracker crumbs, regular or chocolate
- ♥ 3 Tbsp. sugar
- ♥ 3 Tbsp. low-fat margarine, melted
- ♥ 3 - 8 oz. pkgs. fat-free cream cheese, softened
- ♥ 3/4 cup sugar
- ♥ 2 Tbsp. flour
- ♥ 3 Tbsp. lemon juice
- ♥ 3/4 cup egg substitute
- ♥ 1 - 8 oz. carton non-fat peach yogurt

Heat oven to 350°. Mix graham cracker crumbs, 3 Tbsp. sugar and margarine. Pat onto bottom only of 9 or 10-inch springform pan. Set aside. Beat cream cheese, sugar and flour together until light, fluffy and smooth. Gradually add lemon juice and egg substitute; beat well. Add yogurt and mix thoroughly. Pour over prepared crust. Bake for 60-70 minutes or until center of cheesecake is set. Gently run tip of knife along edge of pan. Cool to room temperature before removing from pan. Chill. Serves 12.

GOOEY CINNAMON CAKE

With a little bakery creativity, this is a tasty replica of the fat-laden version

CAKE

2 cups all-purpose flour
1¼ tsp. baking powder
½ tsp. baking soda
½ tsp. ground cinnamon
1 cup non-fat sour cream

⅓ cup each, white sugar and brown sugar
¼ cup egg substitute
3 Tbsp. safflower oil
1 tsp. vanilla extract

TOPPING

1½ Tbsp. sugar   ½ tsp. ground cinnamon

For cake: Preheat oven to 350°. Spray an 8" x 8" baking pan with non-stick vegetable spray. Set aside.

In a medium bowl, mix flour, baking powder, baking soda and cinnamon. Stir well. In a large bowl, mix sour cream, sugars, egg substitute, oil and vanilla. Stir until well blended. Stir in the flour mixture until thoroughly mixed. Pour the batter into the prepared pan.

With a sifter, evenly sift topping ingredients over top of cake. Bake for 20-25 minutes or until toothpick inserted comes out clean. Cool on wire rack before serving.

Serves: 9.

Old-Fashioned Summertime Lemonade Bars

Crust:

1 1/4 cups flour

1 cup oatmeal, quick cooking

1 cup low-calorie margarine

1/2 cup powdered sugar

Topping:

4 eggs or egg substitute

2 cups sugar or equivalent
   sugar substitute

1 6 oz. can undiluted
   lemonade

1/2 cup flour

1/2 tsp. baking powder

3 Tbsp. powdered sugar

Preheat oven to 350°. Mix crust ingredients and press into bottom of 9" x 13" pan that has been sprayed with non-stick cooking spray. Bake for 17 minutes. Mix together topping. Pour onto crust. Bake for another 25-30 minutes until done. Cool well and cut into bars. Sift powdered sugar over the top of bars.

Makes 32 bars.

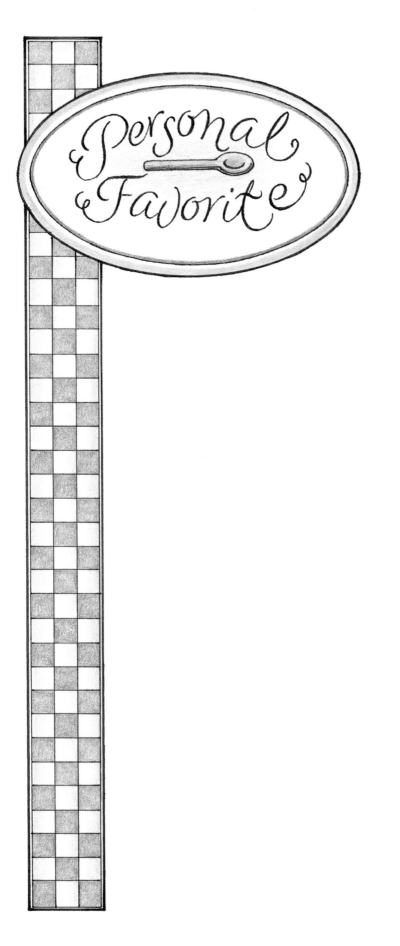

MISCELLANEOUS...

Hot Chocolate

If you're looking for a "healthier than a mix" version of hot chocolate, Look no further. Include your children in the preparation, if they are old enough. This could become a wonderful family tradition for those no-school-snow-day mornings...

1 cup boiling water

scant ¼ cup cocoa

pinch of salt

⅓ cup sugar

3 cups milk, heated

miniature marshmallows for garnish*

Mix cocoa, salt and sugar in a saucepan. Add boiling water and stir to a thin paste. Bring mixture to a boil for 2 minutes, and slowly add warm milk. Stir and heat to desired temperature. Beat with a wire wisk just before serving. Garnish with marshmallows. 4 servings.

 *It is seldom that we associate hot chocolate with spring, but I can recall many Easter mornings that were brisk enough to welcome a piping cup of cocoa... why not top it off with pastel-colored marshmallows as a special Easter tradition?

 Another serving suggestion: follow a Mexican dinner with a cup of cocoa sprinkled with just a little bit of cinnamon.

Hot Fudge Sauce

Excellent for topping
ice cream, pound cake, brownies...
or you may also use this decadent
sauce as a fruit dip. Served
side by side with "Dee's Fruit Dip"
(page 7), it makes a beautiful
presentation.

3/4 cup unsweetened cocoa
3/4 cup sugar
3 Tbsp. butter, cut into slices
1/2 cup heavy cream
pinch salt
1 tsp. vanilla

Mix cocoa and sugar together in a
small saucepan. Stir in butter and
cream. Bring to a boil, stirring constantly,
over medium heat. Boil for 30 seconds.
Remove from heat and stir in salt
and vanilla. Makes one cup.
May be
refrigerated
and reheated.

Will keep approximately 3-4 weeks.

The Perfect Cup of Tea

- Bring water to a boil in a teakettle. Pour into your teapot and rinse to warm it. Then discard this water.

- Measure a heaping teaspoon of loose tea leaves for each person you are serving. Place into the teapot.

- Bring more water (8~10 oz. per guest) to boil in kettle and pour into teapot.
  Cover with tea cozy.

- Brew for 4-5 minutes. Stir the tea in the teapot just a bit. Then pour through a small strainer into cups.

- Serve with milk (or cream) if desired.

- You may use a tea infuser instead of putting loose tea directly into the pot, to avoid having to strain the tea at the end. — Enjoy!

LOGAN TRADING Co.
Lemonade

Debby Logan, from the Logan Trading Company in Raleigh, N.C. shares this old-fashioned lemonade recipe with us. For over 25 years the Logans have been providing their customers with the essentials in gardening products. Their three-acre site is complete with an award-winning greenhouse and the largest garden book selection in the Southeast.

1-2 large lemons, scrubbed and quartered
1 gallon water
2 cups sugar
1 Tbsp. citric acid *

Squeeze lemons really well and add juice and peelings to water. Stir in sugar and citric acid and chill. You may alter these ingredients a little to suit your personal taste.

 *Debby suggests you look for citric acid at a local health food store or a food co-op.

Monster Bubbles

Every cookbook ought to have at least one "recipe for fun". This is it. I want to tell you ~ bubbles have changed since we were young. Remember the little plastic bottles and tiny wands that came inside? All the bubbles were the same shape and size. Now we have giant containers filled with "bubble juice" and wands that are shaped like stars and hearts. But one thing has not changed. To really have fun with this sport, you still turn your face up to the sun, gently blow through the wand and smile at the wonder of your creations. Hint: children, cats and dogs, added to this activity, make it even more fun.

Mix together in a large bowl the following ingredients:

2 cups Joy liquid detergent
6 cups water
3/4 cups light corn syrup

...Store in a large plastic container or jug. Pour into a shallow container when ready to use.

To make wands:

Materials needed:
- ♥ 18" pieces of wire (coated coat hangers will do nicely)
- ♥ dowel sticks, with a small hole drilled in the end
- ♥ bright ribbon

Form a wire into the desired "cookie-cutter" shape, bringing both ends of the wire back down to the bottom to insert into the hole of the dowel stick. You may use a small amount of hot glue to secure the wire. Tie a bright ribbon around the stick. These make great party favors, or "tie ons" for birthday packages. Enjoy!

POTTING SOIL Mix

This "recipe" comes to us from
The Suburban Garden Center, in Davenport, Iowa.
It is the largest landscape business in Iowa, and is
fully staffed with proffessionals who concentrate on
the multifaceted concerns of the homeowner.
The Garden Center not only meets the outdoor needs for
your home, but some of the inside needs as well.
Our visit there to do a book signing in 1993 was
inspirational! If you can't make it to Iowa for a
visit to the Center, "bring it on home", by mixing up
some of their potting mix... this is especially nice for
outdoor container plants.

    4 parts topsoil
    2 parts composted cow manure
    1 part mushroom compost
    1 part sharp sand

For fertilizer: ½ cup lawn "starter fertilizer" —
    sprinkle liberally on top if mixture and work into soil.

A Word About the Bird...

(Rules for Handling Chicken Safely.)

ONE   Store properly. Store in the refrigerator and use within 1-2 days of purchase, or place a second layer of foil or freezer wrap around store packaging and freeze for up to six months. Defrost in refrigerator, not on the countertop... or in the microwave, when in a hurry (about 10 minutes per pound on defrost setting.

❧

TWO   Handle with care. Wash your hands before and after touching raw chicken. Clean all work surfaces and utensils that chicken comes in contact with thoroughly, before putting other foods on them.

❧

THREE   Marinate only in the refrigerator. Then, if you wish to use marinade as a dipping sauce, boil first for at least three minutes.

❧

FOUR   Never stuff ahead of time — this allows for growth of bacteria.

❧

FIVE   Serve promptly. Refrigerate leftovers as soon as possible. If chicken was stuffed, remove stuffing and refrigerate it separately.

❧

Around the House...
(Solutions and Suggestions for)

Homemade Window Cleaner Recipe
♥

Combine ½ cup ammonia, ½ cup isopropyl alcohol rubbing alcohol, and ½ cup water. Put the mixture in a spray bottle and label it clearly. If you like, you can add a few drops of food coloring.

Remove Waterline Marks...
♥

in the toilet bowl by pouring in 2 cups white vinegar. Let soak overnight; flush clean.

White Spots on Wood Furniture?
♥

Combine equal parts of white toothpaste and baking soda. Using a clean, damp cloth, gently rub the mixture into the spot, then buff with a clean dry cloth; polish lightly if necessary.

♥

Many women have found themselves with a collection of shoulder pads that don't seem to go with any of their blouses or sweaters... sort of the same problem as the "one sock syndrome". Use the odd shoulder pads as shoe savers!

Protect Your Cookbooks...

If you don't happen to own an acrylic cookbook stand, an inexpensive substitute is a gallon-sized clear plastic bag. Just slip your cookbook inside and keep it free of spills and spatters.

SRS

144

Index

Thank you
to our many readers
who have expressed an interest
in our other products.

Among Friends offers an extensive line of greeting cards,
note cards, and a variety of stationery items.
For the location of a retailer near you,
please call us at our toll-free number
Monday-Friday 9 a.m.-5 p.m. CST
1-800-377-3566